Philip Spencer Gregory

Records of the Family of Gregory

Philip Spencer Gregory

Records of the Family of Gregory

ISBN/EAN: 9783337022198

Printed in Europe, USA, Canada, Australia, Japan

Cover: Foto ©ninafisch / pixelio.de

More available books at **www.hansebooks.com**

Not Published

Records

of the

Family of Gregory

MDCCCLXXXVI

PRINTED BY VEALE, CHIFFERIEL & CO.
31 TO 37 CURSITOR STREET, CHANCERY LANE, LONDON, E.C.

PREFACE.

THE object of the following pages is to preserve the Genealogical Records of our family for the information of any members or connections of it who may now or hereafter feel an interest in the history of their progenitors. Although no attempt is made to magnify those instances of hereditary qualities which have attracted the attention of the curious in such matters,* these " Records " are not intended to fall into the hands of readers who have no personal interest in the subject.

The appropriateness of the present time for the collection of our genealogical information will be apparent. The snapping of the final link connecting us with the soil of Scotland, and the extinction of one distinct branch of our family, have been almost simultaneous with the re-opening of communications between the members of the family resident in the United Kingdom and their hitherto unknown, but undoubted, relatives in the United States. Again, the recent appearance of three works † in which our name has received very honourable mention has aroused a fresh interest amongst us in genealogical questions.

The documentary evidence from which the following information has been extracted consists principally of a collection of deeds, diplomas, and letters, dating from the middle of the seventeenth century, which has been preserved at Edinburgh. It has been considered that the printing of continual references

---

* See Galton's *Hereditary Genius*, &c., &c.

† Sir A. Alison's *Autobiography*, Sir A. Grant's *Story of the University of Edinburgh*, and Irving's *Eminent Doctors*.

to the authorities for the facts stated would be an unnecessary expense, and therefore, except in special cases, such references are omitted, although no statement is made without sufficient authority. Many of the earlier facts are based upon a fragmentary family history compiled by Dr. James Gregorie of Aberdeen (the elder of the two of that name), at the beginning of the last century; and much supplementary information has been obtained from a more complete (but still imperfect) *Genealogical Sketch*, written in 1826, by Mr. Donald Gregory. The numerous notices of members of the family in the Dictionaries of Biography, and other works of reference, have supplied other information, while many details have been extracted from more general works dealing with life in Scotland during the last two centuries. Some searches have been made in the Register House in Edinburgh; and much benefit has been derived in the researches as to modern times from the Scotch plan of recording deeds, &c., and of "serving" the heir of a deceased person. The earlier periods present, as will be seen, greater difficulties, and the reader must use his or her own discretion as to the amount of credit to be given to the more remote stages in our alleged descent, through the Chiefs of Glenurquhay, from the wearers of the Scottish Crown.

It may be added that as few details as possible are given of living persons.

P. S. G.

2 GLEDHOW GARDENS, S.W.
March 1886.

Contents.

PRELIMINARY CHAPTER.

ON THE SPELLING OF THE NAME GREGORY ... 1

CHAPTER I.

THE MACGREGORS OF GLENURQUHAY—
    THE DESCENT FROM A.D. 882–1415, FOURTEEN GENERATIONS ... 3

CHAPTER II.

THE MACGREGORS OF GLENLYON AND OF RORO—
    A.D. 1415–1515, THREE GENERATIONS ... 9

CHAPTER III.

THE GREGORIES—
    REV. JOHN GREGORIE. THE ANDERSONS. PROFESSOR ANDERSON, OF PARIS. MURDER OF ALEXANDER GREGORIE. DAVID GREGORIE, OF KINAIRDY. PROFESSOR ALEXANDER INNES. PROFESSOR REID, D.D. PROFESSOR JAMES GREGORIE, INVENTOR OF THE REFLECTING TELESCOPE. GEORGE JAMESON, "THE VANDYKE OF SCOTLAND" ... 11

CHAPTER IV.

THE OXFORD BRANCH—
    PROFESSOR DAVID GREGORY. PROFESSOR DAVID GREGORY *Secundus* (*Dean of Christ Church*) ... 30

CHAPTER V.

THE AMERICAN BRANCH—
    PROFESSOR JAMES GREGORIE, OF EDINBURGH, *Secundus* ... 38

Chapter VI.

THE ST. ANDREW'S BRANCH—　　　　　　　　　PAGE
　　Professor Charles Gregorie. Professor David Gregorie *Tertius*　41

Chapter VII.

THE DUNKIRK BRANCH　　　　　　　　　　　43

Chapter VIII.

THE ABERDEEN AND EDINBURGH BRANCH—
　　Professor James Gregorie, M.D., *Tertius*. Principal Chalmers. Professor Campbell. Professor James Gregorie, M.D., *Quartus*. Professor John Gregory, M.D. Professor W. P. Alison, M.D. Sir A. Alison. Professor James Gregory, M.D., *Quintus*. Professor William Gregory. Duncan Farquharson Gregory　　　　　　　45

Chapter IX.

THE ABERDEEN AND EDINBURGH BRANCH (*continued*)—
　　Rev. William Gregory. Dean James Gregory. George Gregory, M.D. John Gregory, *Governor of the Bahamas*　74

Supplementary Chapter.

THE ARMORIAL BEARINGS　　　　　　　　　87

RECORDS OF THE FAMILY OF GREGORY.

PRELIMINARY CHAPTER.

ON THE SPELLING OF THE NAME GREGORY.*

IN the earliest family documents in which the name of Gregorie occurs (1634, 1649, &c.), the name terminates with "ie," but we find that no particular mode of spelling was rigidly adhered to until a comparatively late date.

Thus, in the Letters Patent of Charles II. (in 1669) granting the Professorship at St. Andrew's to James Gregorie, the name is spelt Gregory, while the notarial act of admission following the patent adopts the other mode, and the same Professor's commission to London in 1673 is addressed to him as James Gregory.

David Gregory, the Savilian Professor at Oxford (1691-1708), seems to have adopted the "y" spelling, at all events on migrating to England, and that mode was continued by his descendants.

James Gregorie (David's next brother) obtained a patent for an invention in 1701, in the name of Gregory, although his children's births at Edinburgh, of a later date, are registered with the "ie" termination.

Dr. James Gregorie, the first professor of the family at Aberdeen, adopted the "y" spelling on taking his degree at Rheims, in 1698, and in a contract of sale in 1715; whereas the alternative mode is found in his "retour" as heir to his father in 1690, his "burgess ticket" dated 1706, and the documents relating to his appointment as professor in 1725, and was used by him in signing his son's diploma in 1728. The same Dr. James signed his testamentary dispositions (1730) in the older "ie" form; but confirmation of them using the "y" spelling, in reference to the testator, was granted to his son as Dr. James Gregorie.

The latter "y" form appears again in documents relating to the brothers James and John in 1743 and 1749, and John's note-book of the year 1738 bears his name spelt with a "y"; but with these

---

* See also Note, p. 11.

exceptions, James seems to have adhered to the spelling "Gregorie" down to his death 1755, and John down to the same year.

Except that the appointments of Dr. John Gregory, as professor in Aberdeen (1755), and Edinburgh (1766), were made out in the name of Gregorie, the "y" spelling has been continuously used by Dr. John Gregory and his descendants, from 1755 to the present time.

Some remarkable evidence as to the spelling of the name has recently come to light in the records of the Aberdeen Musical Society, kindly produced to the writer by its president, Mr. James Walker, 52 Union Street, Aberdeen. It appears that Dr. John Gregory was one of the founders of this society in 1747, and for many years held the office of President. His signature to the proceedings from 1747 to 1754, when he migrated to London, is uniformly "Jo. Gregorie": after his return to Aberdeen, viz., in 1757, his signature reappears in the minute-book, and thenceforward is without exception "Jo. Gregory."

It would seem that this visit to England, or rather abortive settlement there, had the same effect upon Dr. John Gregory's mode of spelling his name which it had had upon the only other branch of the family, which had already settled in that country, viz., Professor David Gregory and his descendants. One may, perhaps conjecture that as the name of Gregory was not an uncommon one in the south, it was considered expedient to adopt the spelling usually adopted there, rather than a variation which it might be impossible to perpetuate.

The spelling "Gregorie," however, still survives in the descendants, resident in England, of Professor Charles Gregorie, and it has, perhaps more naturally, been adhered to by the branch of the family settled at Dunkirk.

In considering a possible return on the part of the members of the family now using the "y" spelling to the other form "ie," we have to remember that the name in its present shape as derived from the "Macgregors" was probably used for the first time towards the end of the sixteenth century, and that we have no evidence of the exclusive use of the "ie" form at any time. What we, in fact, have before us, is the unvarying use of the "y" form for 130 years (1755-1885), preceded by a period of 86 years only (1669-1755), during which the two spellings seem to have been used somewhat promiscuously.

CHAPTER I.

The Macgregors of Glenurquhay.

HIGHLAND genealogy is notoriously a complicated and perplexing subject, and probably there is no example of it in which the enquirer is likely to be met with more difficulties and discouragements than in endeavouring to unravel the history of the family or clan of the Macgregors. From 1603 to 1775, with only a short interval of 30 years soon after the Restoration, the name of Gregor, or Macgregor, was proscribed under pain of death, and this circumstance alone is sufficient to account for a considerable failure of genealogical information, there being no reason for persons to search out and preserve proofs of their connection with the proscribed clan, but rather the reverse. Another cause of obscurity in this case is also the admitted fact that the Macgregors persistently clung to the allodial tenure of their lands, and struggled against the imposition of the feudal land system which the Government attempted to force on the country in the fifteenth and sixteenth centuries. Hence the absence of charters which would supply that evidence of genealogy which is the most valuable and interesting.

In 1769, however, we find that Mr. John Murray, who afterwards became by creation Sir John Macgregor-Murray, Bart., prepared an elaborate history of the clan, and communicated it to Sir Robert Douglas for insertion in his *Baronage of Scotland*, then in course of preparation. In making this communication, Mr. Murray made a condition that the history should be published as drawn up by him without alteration, and to this Sir R. Douglas assented; and it was so published accordingly. This condition was probably due to the fact that Mr. Murray's family were personally interested in a dispute as to the chiefship of the clan, which seems to have lasted for nearly a century, and to have been contested with considerable energy on both sides.

Before submitting his account of the clan to Sir R. Douglas, Mr. Murray thought it desirable to obtain the consent of certain prominent persons likely to be affected by it, and, amongst others, of Dr. John Gregory, who is mentioned in the account as descended from the "Ruadrudh" or "Roro" branch of the clan. Although the actual chain of descent of the Gregory family from the main line of the Gregorian chiefs is not given in detail in this *Baronage Account*, the connection is indicated as existing through Gregor, the fourth son of Gregor "Aulin," who is said to have died in 1415.

The dispute already referred to as to the chiefship of the clan became, of course, a burning question upon the removal of the proscription in the year 1775, when the clan was again enabled to claim public recognition of its existence. The contest was practically terminated in 1822 by the acceptance of Sir Evan Macgregor—the son of Sir John—as chief by 2,650 members of the clan "capable of bearing arms," who signed a document to that effect presented to the chief at a public dinner of clansmen at Edinburgh. On this occasion, Lieutenant Gregory, R.E., grandson of Dr. John Gregory before mentioned, acted as "croupier"; and upon a Clan-Gregor Society being founded, for the benefit and mutual assistance of members of the clan in honour of its re-establishment, Mr. Donald Gregory, another grandson of Dr. John Gregory, was appointed its first secretary.

These marks of recognition of the Gregory family as members of the clan may be supplemented by reference to the well-known story of Rob Roy's attempt, on the score of kinship, to obtain Dr. James Gregorie, of Aberdeen, as an associate in his somewhat nefarious enterprises, of which a fuller account will be given in connection with Dr. James Gregorie himself. In the records of the Gregory family we find the tradition of descent from the Macgregors of Roro carefully preserved, but without any very definite evidence in support of it, or even any explicit statement of details.

Notwithstanding the general recognition of Sir Evan Macgregor as chief, he seems to have employed or encouraged Mr. Donald Gregory and another clansman, the Rev. William Macgregor Stirling, to investigate the history of the clan with, apparently, a twofold object, viz. :—(1) to clear the character of the clan from the imputation of lawlessness and atrocity, which gathered round it during its proscription; and (2) to establish the genealogical connections of the different branches of the clan.

As regards the first object (which does not intimately concern the Gregory family, who had settled in the Lowlands before the proscription) the research has made out, that the moral responsibility for the lawless proceedings of the clan rests upon the Government, which, in pursuance of its policy of imposing the feudal system, first granted away the Macgregor lands by charter to favourites of its own, and then endeavoured by penal enactments, commissions of fire and sword, and other violent measures to evict the existing tenants. The defence of the clan upon these grounds will be found in a printed essay published by Donald Gregory in 1831, entitled, *An Inquiry into the History of the Clan Gregor, preceding the Year 1603*.

The second or genealogical branch of the inquiry is more interesting. The conclusions arrived at by Mr. Donald Gregory and his colleague are contained in bulky MSS., of which a summary only is necessary or possible for the present purpose.

The Clan Gregor, it appears, was not certainly known as a *clan* in early times, but rather as a private and quiet *family*, whose chiefs were styled of Glenurquhay or Glenurchy, a district in the Perthshire Highlands between Lochawe and Loch Tay, in which the clan principally, if not originally, resided. In fact, the name Macgregor seems to have been more of a patronymic than a surname until quite recent times—the grandson of a Gregor being commonly designated Vc Gregor.*

Some confusion has arisen as to the position of the chief of the Macgregors of Glenurquhay. The *Baronage Account* states broadly, on the authority of a Latin MS. discovered at the Scots College, Paris, that Sir Malcolm Macgregor (who died in 1164) was raised to "the peerage" as Lord Macgregor, in recognition of an act of bravery in saving the life of his sovereign, David I. But at this time the peerage in its later form had not become part of the Constitution of Scotland, and the title conferred upon Sir Malcolm Macgregor would appear to have been that of "Mor'air" or "great man"—a title borne by those who were made superintendents or lieutenants of the districts which they held allodially,

* *See* Note, p. 11.

such offices becoming ultimately hereditary. Sir Malcolm Macgregor, therefore, became Mor'air de Glenurquhay; and this title was borne by his descendants until the ultimate loss of Glenurquhay itself about the year 1440.

After criticising the evidence on the subject (which includes the "Lyslebourg" MS. in the British Museum, called *Scotica Nobilitas*, 1509, and containing a list of the barons of Scotland) Mr. Stirling states the following results: "It is most likely that the chiefs of Glenurquhay had very early held the rank of earl, although the Gaelic word for it had never in technical phrase been rendered by its correspondent one. Further, that a Gregorian chief was a party in a public instrument at the end of the thirteenth century as a great baron by tenure, then next to earl, is certain; and that another had, in the reign of either James I. or James II., attained, by whatever process then in use, the rank of baron by creation or lord of Parliament is, we conceive, a proposition resting on as good evidence as in the peculiar circumstances of the case, can reasonably be demanded."

It may be mentioned in this connection, as indicating the great possibility of confusion between the territorial and non-territorial titles, that David Gregorie, of Kinairdy, who died in 1720, is spoken of in a document about 67 years later as "Baron of Kinairdy."

The Macgregor title and any privileges which were annexed to it seem to have been lost to the family, together with the territory with which it was originally connected.

Returning to the Macgregor pedigree as given in the *Baronage*, we find that while it follows the elder line of the descent, the families of Grant, Robert Bruce, Baliol, Stewart, spring from younger branches of the same stem. As to the earlier part of the pedigree (which will be presently set out) no complaint is made by Mr. Donald Gregory or Mr. Stirling against the *Baronage Account*, except that the original forefather from whom descent is traced is elevated in the more recent account to the dignity of a king, whereas, according to the *Baronage*, he did not come to the throne. The serious fault found by the later enquirers is with the descent from William of Glenurquhay, who died in 1238.

The genealogy, so far as made out from the papers already referred to, works out into the following table of fourteen generations in a direct line extending over more than 500 years.

I. GREGOR, son of Dougal, and king of Scots and Picts, A.D. 882-897.

II. DOUGAL, died A.D. 901; married Spontana, sister of Duncan—an Irish king.

III. CONSTANTINE, died A.D. 940; married Malvina, daughter of King Donald IV.

IV. GREGOR NA BRATIC (of the Standard), killed in battle with the Danes, A.D. 961; married Dorvigelda, daughter of The Doorward.

V. JOHN, killed in battle, A.D. 1004; married Alpina, daughter of Angus.

VI. GREGORIUS DE GLENURQUHAY (or GLENURHARD), called Gregor the Stout, and mentioned in the history of the family of Argyll, died A.D. 1060; married a daughter of Paul O'Dhuine, Lord of Lochow.

VII. DOMINUS JOANNES DE GLENURQUHAY, died A.D. 1113; married an English lady. His brother was Bishop of St. Andrew's.

VIII. DOMINUS MALCOLMUS DE GLENURQUHAY, called in the songs of the bards "Morer Callum nan Caistal" or "Lord Malcolm of the Castles," died A.D. 1164; married Marjory, daughter of The Doorward, Earl of Moray, and son of King Duncan II. His brother was Bishop of Dunkeld.

IX. WILLIAM DE GLENURQUHAY, died A.D. 1238; married a lady of the house of Lindsay.

X. JOHN GLENDOCHIR, a younger son of the above, on 3rd March 1238 was witness to a charter.

XI. MALCOLM DE GLENDOCHART, afterwards of Glenurquhay, swore fealty to Edward I. on 2nd August 1276, and was wounded at the battle of Dundalk, 1318; married Mary daughter of Malcolm M'Alpin.

XII. GREGORIUS DE GLENURQUHAY.

XIII. JOHN CHAM MACGREGOR ("One-eyed John") died in Glenurquhay, and was buried in Dysart on the north side of the High Altar, 19th April 1390, as mentioned in *Dean Macgregor's Chronicle*.

XIV. GREGOR M'ANECHAM, or AULIN (the handsome), died in Glenurquhay, and was buried as above, A.D. 1415; as mentioned in *Dean Macgregor's Chronicle*. He married Iric, daughter of Malcolm M'Alpin.

It will be seen that information as to the last two generations in the foregoing table is derived from *Dean Macgregor's Chronicle*. This was an old manuscript preserved in the archives of the Highland Society, and published by Mr. Donald Gregory in the

Archæologica Scotica in 1831. It contains an obituary in Latin of Highland notabilities, apparently the work of Sir James Macgregor, who was Dean of Lismore about 1550.

Mr. Donald Gregory's chief objection to the *Baronage Account* is based upon its omission of all reference to the Macgregors of Glenlyon, from which, it would seem, that the Roro branch is descended. This omission is supplied in the following account, which is taken from Mr. Macgregor Stirling's MS. already referred to, and may be accepted as the result of the joint labours of himself and Mr. Donald Gregory.

CHAPTER II.

THE MACGREGORS OF GLENLYON AND OF RORO.

I.* GREGOR, the fourth son of Gregor M'Anecham, No. XIV and last in the preceding table,† was the allodial proprietor of Glenlyon, a district in Perthshire adjacent to Glenurquhay, and had two sons:—

    1. John, called "John Dhu nan Lann," or "Black John of the Spears," who died in his 99th year without leaving any surviving issue, but having disposed of any right he had to Glenlyon in favour of one of the Campbells of Glenurquhay.‡

    2. Duncan, of whom below.

II. Duncan, who appears to have been designated "Lienoch" (i.e., "from Glenlyon"), and to have been surnamed Beg, or "little," founded the family of the Macgregors of Roro. This individual is referred to in a bailbond given by the clan to the Earl of Argyll, and dated 22nd April 1601, as the ancestor of several of the parties to the bond; and his death at Roro, on the 17th February 1477, is recorded in *Dean Macgregor's Chronicle.* He is said to have married Elizabeth, daughter of the Laird Macnaughten of Dundaramh.

Duncan Beg Lienoch left five sons :—

    1. Gregor, of whom below.
    2. Allaster Mor, ancestor of the Macgregors of Balhaldies.
    3. John Moill Duncanson.
    4. Duncan Dhu, ancestor of the Macgregors of Leragan.
    5. Malcolm.

---

* For convenience the generations are numbered from this point.   † Page 7.

‡ The Campbells had acquired Glenurquhay by charters from the Crown, and had evicted the Macgregors.

III. Gregor, the eldest son of Duncan of Roro, and hence called "Duncanson," is mentioned in *Dean Macgregor's Chronicle* as having died at Roro in April 1515, and having been buried at Killin. He is the hero of an ancient Gaelic ballad, in which reference is made to his "right to Glenlyon," of which he was deprived by his uncle's alienation mentioned above.

Gregor Duncanson is said to have married a daughter of Sir Robert Menzies of Weem, and to have had five sons:—

1. Duncan.
2. Neill.
3. James.
4. John Cam.
5. Malcolm.

CHAPTER III.

THE GREGORIES.

THE point which has now been reached in tracing the family history is that at which help is first obtained from the records of the family of Gregorie itself. Apart from documents of a public or legal character, these records consist of a family history compiled by Dr. James Gregorie, of Aberdeen, early in the eighteenth century, and of the letters of Dr. Reid, of Glasgow, who in his later years communicated to his relative, Dr. James Gregory, of Edinburgh, the reminiscences of his early life concerning his maternal ancestry. Upon these materials the history can be proceeded with as follows :—

IV. James Macgregor, third son of Gregor Duncanson, settled on the Boyne, a district near the town of Banff, about 1510. He married a lady who was daughter of the Laird of Findlater (Ogilvie), and a relative of Lord Findlater, and by her he had a family of ten sons and a daughter, a record being preserved of only the following :—

1. James, of whom below.
2. Thomas, who is mentioned in his brother's will as one of his creditors, and died without issue.
3. Janet.

V. James, surnamed "Gregorie,"* was by his relative, Findlater, made his "chamberlain" at Woodland, in the parish of Udnie, in Aberdeenshire. He married Agnes, sister of William

---

* No authentic explanation is forthcoming of the adoption of this name; obviously it was not due to the proscription of the name Macgregor, first proclaimed in 1603. Dr. James Gregorie's *Family History* states that the surname "Gregorie" was assumed "as an equivalent for Macgregor," and it has been conjectured that on the Highland Macgregor settling in the lowlands of Aberdeenshire, where Gaelic was not spoken, he adopted the southern termination "ie" as an equivalent in meaning to the Gaelic "Mac" (son). There was, in fact, no actual *change*. As stated above (p. 5), the name Macgregor was not a surname in the modern sense of the word, and was adopted merely as a description. Thus James (No. IV. above) was properly called Macgregor, being the son of Gregor Duncanson, but his son James (No. V.) would have been more correctly styled Vegregor, *i.e.* son of Macgregor. This nomenclature would have sounded strange in the ears of Lowlanders, and it may well be that although the family of Macgregors were not then under the ban of proscription, their more peaceful relative settling in

More (or Moir), Laird of Ferryhill, near Aberdeen, and, dying in December 1584, left the following children who survived him, besides others who pre-deceased him, viz. :—

1. James.
2. Thomas, who died without issue.
3. Janet.

VI. James Gregorie, was a saddler in Aberdeen, and several times held the office of Deacon-Convener of the "incorporated trades" in that city. It may be explained that each of the "trades" is presided over by a deacon, and that the head of all the trades is termed the Deacon-Convener. The saddlers were included in the trade of the Hammermen.*

James Gregorie married Margaret Barber (or Barbour), a merchant's daughter, by whom he had two sons :—

1. John, of whom below, who was served heir to his father, 27th May 1623.†
2. James, a merchant in Aberdeen, who married Marjory Tough, and by her left one surviving daughter, Margaret, who died, unmarried, at Aberdeen, aged 70, in 1701.

VII. The Reverend John Gregorie, born 1598, died 1650.

Mr. John Gregorie was educated at schools in Aberdeen, and at the Marischal College there, and afterwards studied theology at St. Andrew's University. In 1620, Mr. Gregorie was appointed Minister of Drumoak, a parish in Deeside (Aberdeenshire), and in the following year he married Janet, second daughter of David Anderson, of Finzeach, or Finiach. The Andersons‡ appear to have been a family of remarkable talent ; one of them, a near relative of Mrs. Gregorie, was Professor of Mathematics at Paris early in the

---

Aberdeenshire was quite willing to adopt the customs of his neighbours in regard to surnames, and to give up a practice of nomenclature which would at once recall his connection with his more lawless clansmen among the hills. The diminutive of Gregor, formed by the addition of "ie," as in familiar instances, was taken as a surname. It may be noticed, in illustration, that in Greek some forms of patronymics and diminutives are practically identical : ($δης — διον$).

* *See Inscriptions on the Shields of the Incorporated Trades*, by Jervise ; Aberdeen, 1863.
† *See Aberdeen Burgh Records*, II., 385.   ‡ *See* the accompanying "Anderson Pedigree."

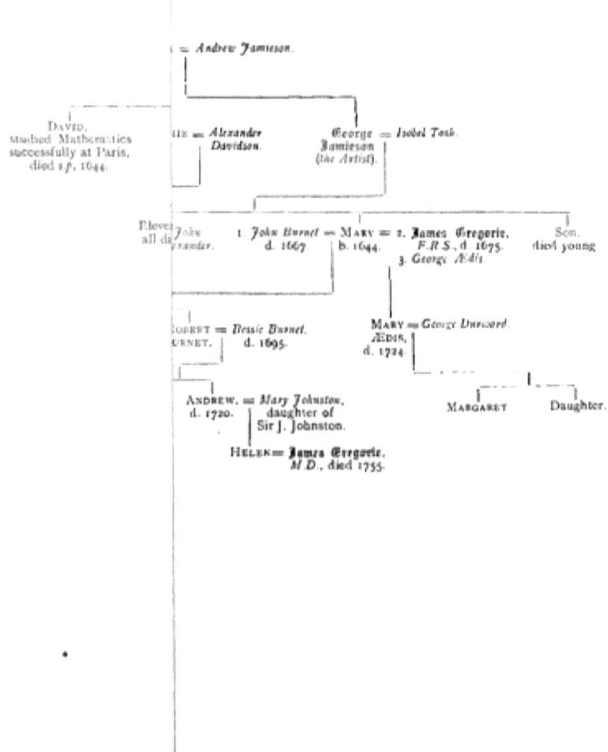

seventeenth century, and published several mathematical works. David Anderson himself is mentioned as possessing "great mechanical genius" in the *Book of Bon-Accord*, 279-280, and in the *History of Scots Affairs*, written in 1659-1661 and published by the Spalding Society. It appears that Mrs. Gregorie inherited a taste for mathematics, and herself gave her sons early instruction in that subject. Some tapestry of her work is preserved at the back of the Magistrates' Gallery in the West Church at Aberdeen.*

Dr. William Guild, half-brother of Mrs. Gregorie's mother, was Principal of King's College, Aberdeen; and David Anderson, a grandson of Dr. William Guild's sister, was Professor of Theology in the same college in 1712.

According to the *History of Scots Affairs*, already referred to, Mr. John Gregorie was a "riche man," and being "of the moderate party in the Church," in the troubles of his period he, not unnaturally, soon drew upon himself the attacks of the opposite party. For his "outstanding against the Covenant" he was fined 1,000 merks and was dragged to prison with every circumstance of cruelty and insult.† In 1639, in company with some of his colleagues in the ministry, he fled by sea from Aberdeen before Montrose's advance, and was brought back by Lord Aboyne and the Royalist force.‡

In 1640, Mr. Gregorie was deprived of his benefice by the Assembly of Aberdeen; but he was restored by that of St. Andrew's in 1641. His restoration is stated by Spalding to have been effected through the influence of the Laird of Drum, who claimed him as his "awin pastour," and upon his "sueiring and subscriving the Covenant and teaching penitentialle."

His recantation seems to have been considered satisfactory by his neighbours, for we find that in 1642 Mr. Gregorie was elected a commissioner to represent the Aberdeen Presbytery at the Assembly at St. Andrew's of that year. But an anecdote recorded by Spalding shows that his sermons sometimes contained doctrines of a High Church tendency, or at least antagonistic to the Kirk

---

* *Statistical Account of Scotland.* † *See Spalding's History of the Troubles in Scotland.*
‡ *Burton's History of Scotland.*

rules, and brought him into collision with his colleagues. The quarrel preserved by the historian was, fortunately, not too serious to be made up over a "coup of wine."

In 1644, Mr. Gregorie's worldly possessions were further increased by the death of his brother-in-law, David Anderson, without issue; upon that event, the estate of Finzeach (which was in the parish of Monymusk, Aberdeenshire) and other real property devolved upon Mrs. Gregorie and her two sisters as co-heiresses. Mr. Gregorie was, however, destined to become a landed proprietor on a more extensive scale, and, as it turned out, rather from necessity than choice. It appears that he had become a creditor, probably for money lent, of James Crichton of Kinairdy, and his eldest son, James, who, in 1642, had been created Viscount Frendraught. The insolvency of these persons led to legal proceedings, as a result of which, in 1647, the estates of Frendraught in Aberdeenshire, and Kinairdy and Netherdaill in Banffshire, were made over to Mr. Gregorie in satisfaction of his debt, which, with interest, &c., then amounted to the sum of 62,538 merks, or nearly £3,600 sterling—a large sum for those days. Although, as will hereafter appear, these estates did not remain long in the family, their holding had such an important influence on the family, and their names are so closely connected with some of its members that it may be not uninteresting to quote the following description of them contained in the *Statistical Account of Scotland*:

> "Parish of Marnoch (formerly Aberchirder), a little below (the Bridge over the Doveron) stands the old tower-looking mansion of Kinardy, on a promontory at the junction of the burn of the same name with the Doveron. The situation is peculiarly picturesque and commanding. This house is very ancient, has been built at various periods and was together with much of the property of the parish held by the Crichtons of Frendraught, whose chief residence of Frendraught was in the neighbouring parish of Forgue. The river then winds its way towards the church manse and village of Inverkeithny, on the opposite bank about two miles distant. A little lower down are the grounds and mansion house of Netherdale, the property of Mrs. Rose-Innes second heritor of the parish. The house is modern and handsome."

The property of Kinairdy now belongs to Lord Fife.

A memorial of Mr. John Gregorie and his wife still remains at Aberdeen, in a charitable foundation for the education and maintenance of orphans "within the said burgh," which was established by the Anderson family, including Mrs. Gregorie, in 1647. The property appropriated for this good purpose consisted, besides £300 in money, of "the Blackfriars Manse" situate at the School-Hill of Aberdeen, of which, however, Mrs. Anderson, mother of Mrs. Gregorie, retained possession during her life, paying rent to the charity. It may be observed that poor kinsfolk of David Anderson and his sisters have a preference in respect of this institution.

Mr. John Gregorie died and was buried at Drumoak, in 1650. The present writer visited the locality in October 1884, but was unsuccessful in finding any clue to the identity of Mr. John Gregorie's grave in the old churchyard. The old parish church, with its manse, now commonly called Dalmaock, stands close to the river Dee, which, in fact, is making rapid encroachments upon the churchyard. The church is a ruin, and the manse is used as a farmhouse, a new church and manse having been built more in the centre of the parish of Drumoak. The present Mr. Alexander Irvine of Drum, told the writer that he had attended service in the old church, and remembered the tombstone of Mr. John Gregorie; as, however, the tombstones are nearly all of a slatey character, the effacement of the inscription is not a matter for surprise.

Dr. Fraser, Minister of Drumoak, writing in 1805 to Dr. James Gregory, says that he could not find the slightest tradition of "old Mr. Gregorie" in the parish, and that the parish records then extant began in 1670.

Mr. John Gregorie had five children:—
1. Alexander, his heir.
2. David, of whom below, p. 17.
3. James, ,, ,, p. 21.
4. Margaret, who married Thomas Mercer, merchant in Aberdeen, and had issue.
5. Janet, who married Thomas Thomson of Faichfield, and had issue. Amongst her descendants is Mr. Alexander Irvine of Drum, already referred to.

VIII. Alexander Gregorie, born 1623, died 1664.

Alexander Gregorie, the eldest son of the Rev. John Gregorie, was served heir to his father 31st March 1651. Some time before the year 1657 he appears to have entered into an arrangement with his mother, by which he made over to her various parts of his father's Crichton estates, in exchange for her third share of the Finzeach property. In 1660 Mrs. Gregorie divided the property thus acquired by her amongst her younger children, reserving her own life estate, while about the same time Alexander Gregorie sold his share of Finzeach to his relatives, the Wilsons, who were the owners, by descent from the Andersons, of other shares of the same estate.

But the times were not those in which men were content to allow their property to be quietly enjoyed by successors, who had evicted them, however rightfully. Accordingly, we find that Alexander Gregorie and the other owners of the foreclosed Crichton estates suffered so much molestation and annoyance from the Crichton family, that in 1660 they were compelled to demand the protection of the law from the Committee of Estates. James, second Viscount Frendraught, and his followers, were outlawed for non-appearance when summoned before the Committee, and were only relieved upon giving security (in a bond of £40,000 Scots, or £333 6s. 8d. sterling) to keep the peace and to appear before the Privy Council to answer the charges made against them.

The feud between the former proprietors of the Frendraught estates and their new owners was not, however, terminated by this measure, and several further bonds are still extant given on both sides as security against breaches of the peace or disturbance of possession. At last, on the 7th March 1664, a climax was reached in a treacherous and murderous attack being made upon Alexander Gregorie during a friendly ride near Bognie (30 miles from Aberdeen), by Francis Crichton (Frendraught's uncle), and his servant. A few days later Alexander Gregorie succumbed to the wounds he received in this encounter, and the brutal treatment which, in his wounded condition, he received at the hands of his cowardly assailants.

James Crichton, of Kinairdy (who, as related in the *History of the Earldom of Sutherland*, was already notorious for his complicity in the murder of William Gordon, of Rothiemay), and his grandson, Viscount Frendraught, were, together with Francis, the principal in this affair, indicted for the murder of Alexander Gregorie. Francis Crichton, being a Catholic, and, as such, favoured by the Duke of York, obtained a postponement of the trial on the allegation that the murdered man had died from some cause other than the alleged violence; and, during the interval, the culprit escaped from the Tolbooth of Edinburgh, where he was confined. His father and nephew were acquitted of complicity in the murder. The prosecution was revived in 1667 against Francis Crichton, but seems not to have been brought to any conclusion, and in 1682, eighteen years after the murder, Francis Crichton obtained a pardon under the Great Seal. He is said to have fallen soon after in an action at sea.

Alexander Gregorie married Jean, daughter of Dr. Ross, minister in Aberdeen. Dying without issue, he was succeeded in the lands of Netherdaill and Kinairdy by his brother, David Gregorie.

VIII. David Gregorie, born 1625, died 1720.

David Gregorie, second son of the Reverend John Gregorie, and commonly known as "David Gregorie of Kinairdy," is remarkable, not only for the length of his life, and the number (which has often been exaggerated in the references to him) of his children, but also for his mathematical and mechanical genius. Accounts of him appear in *Chambers' Dictionary of Biography*, the *Encyclopædia Britannica*, and elsewhere, and he is credited with "all the genius of his family" by Mr. Francis Galton in his work on *Hereditary Genius*. A curious old paper is preserved containing the dates and hours of the day of the birth of his children, as well as other particulars, and appears to be in the handwriting of Professor David Gregory, the eldest of the children who came to full age. Other particulars of David Gregorie are derived from the letters of his grandson, Dr. Reid, to Dr. James Gregory, of Edinburgh.

David Gregorie was born 20th December 1625, and was educated in Holland for mercantile pursuits, but in 1655, soon after his father's death, he relinquished commerce and took up his residence in Aberdeen, where his son David was born in 1659.

At this period he seems to have taken to literary and scientific studies, which he never afterwards abandoned. He was almost entirely self-taught, and to him his younger brother, James, as well as his own children, owed much of their early teaching. From 1663-1669 he held the appointment of Librarian of King's College, although not a graduate of that university. He kept up correspondence with some of his scientific contemporaries, foreign as well as Scotch; amongst the former being Mariotte, with whom he discussed the subject of the Atmospheric Laws, in which he took great interest.

On 20th April 1659, at the Synod of Aberdeen, David Gregorie appears as a deacon, taking part in an election of a minister for Aberdeen (*Eccles. Records of Aberdeen, Spalding Society*, 245). Later in life he became an "Episcopalian," and he is so described by Dr. Reid.

In 1660 his elder brother, Alexander, settled some property (Over Aschalache, &c.) on David Gregorie and his family, subject to the life estate of Mrs. Gregorie, the mother of David and Alexander.

After succeeding to Kinairdy, upon his brother's death, in 1664, David Gregorie resided on that property (which is about 40 miles from Aberdeen) for many years; but in 1690 (according to the *Statistical Account of Scotland*) he settled the estate upon his son Professor David, and then, or soon afterwards, returned to Aberdeen (*Encyclopædia Britannica*).

David Gregorie's scientific and literary attainments and studies gained him the respect of his neighbours, although the latter indulged in a good deal of ridicule of his consequent neglect of his estate. His medical skill, which was considerable, was placed gratuitously at the service of the poor, and, although he was not a physician by profession, he was frequently called in by his wealthier neighbours; but he was consistent in declining to take a fee.

His habits were regular, and, in order to find time for his studies amid the pressure of other work, he used to rise at two or three a.m., and then slept an hour or two after breakfast.

He was the first person in his neighbourhood to possess a barometer—a possession which nearly led to his prosecution before the Presbytery for witchcraft, a deputation of ministers actually calling upon him for explanations of the reports which were circulated of his proceedings.

During Marlborough's wars, David Gregorie turned his attention to the subject of gunnery, and invented an improvement in artillery. A model of this invention he submitted, through his son David, for the opinion of Sir Isaac Newton, who declared that the inventor, whose name was suppressed, deserved punishment rather than reward, as the machine only "tended to the destruction of the human race, and might become known to the enemy." Whether in consequence of this answer or not cannot be stated, but, as a fact, David Gregorie, who, in his keenness to see the effect of his invention, and in spite of his great age, was preparing to join the army in the field in Flanders, abandoned his project and destroyed his model. The clockmaker, who made the parts of it, was never permitted to see the machine complete.

About the year 1715, on the outbreak of the rebellion in that year, David Gregorie carried his family over to Holland, but returned to Aberdeen shortly before his death, which took place in 1720.

A curious indication of his vigour is his prosecution, at the age of ninety-one, of an appeal to the House of Lords (Robertson, A.D. 1716, p. 178), in an action brought against him as overseer under a will, charging him with a devastavit. The appeal was unsuccessful, and David Gregorie was condemned in thirty guineas costs.

David Gregorie was twice married: the first time, 8th February 1655, being to Jean, daughter of Patrick Walker, of Orchiston, merchant in Aberdeen; by that lady (who died October 1671) he had fifteen children,* viz.:—

    1. Jean, born 27th March 1656, died November 1675.
    2. John, born 3rd February 1657, died 21st February 1658.
    3. Alexander, born 24th February 1658, died November 1658.

---

* David Gregorie's family is often stated to have numbered 32, but the details given in the text are taken from the document in the handwriting of his eldest son above referred to, and may be accepted as authentic.

4. David (of whom below), born 3rd June 1659.
5. William, born 12th July 1660, died March 1661.
6. Isabel, born 18th July 1661, married in 1681 to Patrick Innes, of Balnaboth, afterwards of Tillifour, who died in 1697. Her eldest son, John, had a son Alexander, Professor of Philosophy at Marischal College, and a daughter, married to Principal Chalmers,* of Aberdeen.
7. Janet, born 10th August 1662, died unmarried 1686.
8. Christian, born 15th January 1664, married 1694, to John Cuthbert, W.S., in Edinburgh, afterwards of Rosshall, died 12th January 1739.
9. { Margaret, } twins, born 5th Feb. 1665, { Oct. 1667.
   { Marjorie, }   died   { Sept. 1665.
11. James, born 29th April 1666, of whom below.
12. Patrick, born 26th July 1667, died 29th January 1668.
13. A son, stillborn, at Turriff, 13th September 1668.
14. Anna, born 16th February 1670; died October 1675.
15. A daughter, stillborn, October 1671.

On 15th February 1672 David Gregorie married (secondly) Isabel, daughter of John Gordon, bailie and merchant in Aberdeen, and by her had fourteen children. This lady was connected with the family of the Duke of Gordon, and her brother, John Gordon, Provost of Aberdeen, was a most eminent personage in that city.

David Gregorie's first wife (Jean Walker) and her descendants were "all Tories and Episcopalians" according to Dr. Reid; while the second wife and her family were "zealous Presbyterians."

The issue of David Gregorie's second marriage was as follows:
1. Margaret, born 25th March 1673, was married to Mr. Lewis Reid, minister of Strachan, Kincardineshire. She died in 1732, leaving two sons and two daughters. Her youngest son was the Rev. Thomas Reid, D.D., the celebrated metaphysician. His life is given in the *Encyclopædia Britannica*, and a fuller account was published, with his works, by Dugald Stewart. He

---
* See below, page 44.

was born at Strachan, April 1710; elected Professor*
of Philosophy (including mathematics, physics, logic,
and ethics) at King's College, Aberdeen, 1752;
elected Professor of Moral Philosophy at Glasgow,
1763; and died 1796. His principal work was the
Inquiry into the Human Mind. He was a friend of Dr.
John Gregory, and with him, Beattie Campbell and
Gerard, established a literary society at Aberdeen.
2. John (i.), born 23rd June 1674, died 1675.
3. A daughter stillborn, 7th October 1675.
4. Jean, born 1676, was married to James Deans, merchant in Aberdeen, but had no issue.
5. Alexander, born 1678, lost at sea on his way to Holland.
6. John (ii.), born 1679, staple factor at Campvere, who died at Edinburgh.
7. Charles, born 14th February 1681, of whom and his posterity below.
8. Mary, born June 5th 1682, died unmarried.
9. William, born February 2nd 1684, who died a young lad.
10. George, staple factor at Campvere, of whom and his posterity below.
11. Anna, was married to James Bartlet, merchant in Aberdeen and had issue.
12. Robert, died unmarried.
13. Arthur, who died when at college, in 1715.
14. Infant.

Before proceeding with the descendants of David Gregorie of Kinairdy, who form the elder branch of the family, it will be more convenient to introduce an account of Kinairdy's younger brother James, whose great talents and reputation certainly affected the career of his kinsmen to a considerable extent.

VIII. James Gregorie, M.A., F.R.S., born 1638, died 1675.

James Gregorie, the third and youngest son of the Rev. John Gregorie of Drumoak, is entitled to be ranked " as one of the most

---

* Regent.

eminent mathematicians of the seventeenth century," notwithstanding his death at the early age of 36. The evident respect which he obtained at the hands of Newton and Leibnitz and his other scientific contemporaries shows that while it would, no doubt, be presumptuous to compare his reputation with that of either of the mathematicians just named, his powers were of a very high order. A biography of James Gregorie will be found in almost every dictionary of biography, the most complete being that in the *Biographia Britannica*. He was born in November 1638 (according to the *Statistical Account of Scotland*) at Drumoak, but, according to other accounts, at Aberdeen. It is said that his mother, observing in him while yet a child a strong "propensity to mathematics," instructed him herself in the elements of that science. The rest of his education he received at the grammar school at Aberdeen, after leaving which he went through the usual course of studies at the Marischal College, Aberdeen, taking his degree in 1657.

Amongst the students who graduated, or, according to the Scotch phrase, "laureated," at the same time with James Gregorie at the Marischal College was Gilbert Burnet—a member of a well-known Aberdeen family—afterwards Bishop of Salisbury and the author of the *History of the Reformation*.*

James Gregorie seems to have devoted himself entirely to scientific pursuits, and especially to optical researches, and at a very early age (before he was twenty-four) his labours resulted in the invention of the reflecting telescope. Although reflecting telescopes are not in use at the present day, they were for some time in the last century employed at the best observatories, the principle adopted being that formulated by James Gregorie with the improvements in details which were suggested by subsequent inventors.

James Gregorie is said † to have gone up to London to get his instrument executed by the most skilful workmen, and it would seem that his work on optics, to be presently mentioned, which was published in London in 1663, must have been brought out during the visit made for this purpose.

---

* *Biographia Britannica*. † Spalding Society, *Fasti Aberdonenses*.

This work, which was in Latin, is entitled *Optica Promota seu Abdita radiorum reflexorum et refractorum Mysteria Geometricé enucleata ; cui subnectitur Appendix subtilissimorum Astronomiæ Problematon Resolutionem exhibens.* In it James Gregorie described his reflecting telescope, and also made the suggestion, then quite novel, that the transits of Venus and Mercury might be used for determining the solar parallax, upon which is based the method now employed for determining the sun's distance.

The reflecting telescope as designed by James Gregorie was executed by Reeve, the best practical workman of the day, but did not prove a success in his hands. It would seem that the difficulty of obtaining conoidal reflectors was almost insuperable; and this shape, originally indicated by James Gregorie, was afterwards given up in favor of a spherical form when reflecting telescopes were brought into general use by Hadley in 1715. Notwithstanding this initial failure, the invention immediately attracted the attention of the scientific men both of our own and foreign countries, who were soon convinced of its great importance in relation to optics and astronomy. Amongst other friendships which James Gregorie appears to have now obtained amongst scientific men was that of Mr. John Collins, who was the constant medium through which James Gregorie's work was brought before the Royal Society of London, and who, after his death, published an account of his mathematical writings and discoveries.

In 1668, Newton took up the subject of reflecting telescopes, having, as he admits, James Gregorie's book before him ; and, perceiving that the Gregorian mode of placing the two specula or reflectors upon the same axis was attended with the disadvantage of losing the central rays of the large speculum, suggested an improvement by giving an oblique position to the smaller speculum, and placing the eye-glass in the side of the tube. This improved shape is called the Newtonian telescope, and, of course, it is only an improvement or variation upon the Gregorian arrangement ; and no independent invention of the reflecting telescope is claimed by Newton.

The *Encyclopædia Britannica* contains the following passage :—
" It is worth remarking that the Newtonian construction was long

abandoned for the original or Gregorian form which is at this day [1815] universally employed where the instrument is of a moderate size, though Herschell afterwards preferred the Newtonian form for the construction of his immense telescopes."

James Gregorie now seems to have turned his attention to "pure mathematics," the study of which he pursued at Padua, to which city he was attracted by the high reputation in matters of science then enjoyed by its university. There he resided and laboured for some years, and in 1667 produced as the fruits of his investigations a Latin work on the measurement of the areas of curves, entitled *Vera Circuli et Hyperboles Quadratura*. "Few mathematicians," says Professor de Morgan (*Paradoxes* 71), "now read this very abstruse speculation, but at the time of its appearance it created a considerable sensation in the scientific world," and according to Sir A. Grant,[*] it "at once became famous." The object of it was first to show that it was impossible, *geometrically*, to *square*, or ascertain the area of, a circle (or hyperbola), and, secondly, to show that this problem *can* be solved by means of an infinite converging series.

Only a few copies of this work were struck off in 1667 for private use, one copy being communicated by Mr. John Collins to the Royal Society. Mr. Wallis and Lord Brouncker having expressed favourable opinions of it, the work was published in 1668, together with an addition or appendix in which the author replied to the criticisms passed on the principal work. This appendix he called *Geometriæ pars Universalis inserviens Quantitatum Curvarum Transmutationi et Mensuræ*, its principal feature being the indication of an original general method for finding the areas of curves by means of "transmutation," that is, of using some essential property of the curve to change it into another figure equal thereto of known properties. An attempt was made after James Gregorie's death to claim the credit of this invention for French mathematicians; but Dr. David Gregory, the Oxford Professor, satisfactorily disposed of this and defended his uncle's claims to priority.

An account of this treatise was given to the Royal Society of London before its publication by Mr. Collins; and on the 14th

---

[*] *Story of the University of Edinburgh.*

January 1668, its author was elected a Fellow of the Society. From this period he kept up a constant correspondence with Newton, Lord Brouncker, Huygens, Halley, and Wallis, and contributed many papers to the *Philosophical Transactions of the Royal Society*.

The methods adopted by James Gregorie in his *Vera Circuli et Hyberboles Quadratura*, were, however, not allowed to pass unchallenged, and they were, in fact, somewhat severely handled by Huygens in the French *Journal des Savans*. James Gregorie at first replied to these animadversions very temperately and courteously in the *Philosophical Transactions*, candidly confessing to certain errors; but the dispute in time waxed warm, and it must be admitted that James Gregorie showed himself somewhat overzealous for his own reputation as a discoverer. The papers on both sides are reprinted in Huygens' *Opera Varia*, Leyden, 1724.

Leibnitz, while giving James Gregorie the highest merit for his genius and discoveries, has pronounced that Huygens not only pointed out some considerable deficiencies in the treatise objected to, but also showed a much simpler method of attaining the object in view. It is stated,[*] and probably is the fact, that while Gregorie's scheme of work was well founded, his faults were "tediousness, complication, and intricacy."

In 1668, Mr. James Gregorie (having then returned from Italy) published another work, entitled *Exercitationes Geometricæ*, in which he gave two of what we should now call "integrations" of trigonometrical functions, and also demonstrated the connection which had been observed between Wright's "meridional parts" and the logarithms of cotangents, a proposition on which the construction of Mercator's chart depends. About this time he also produced "*Gregorie's Series*"—a proposition which, in a slightly altered form, was claimed by Leibnitz as his own invention; but luckily for James Gregorie's reputation, Leibnitz's own confession of his appropriation of the labours of the former has been preserved.

It is curious to note that in 1669 James Gregorie's works were suppressed in Italy,[†] but on what ground does not appear.

---

[*] *Biographia Britannica*.   [†] Letter to Collins, 6th January 1670.

In 1669, James Gregorie married (in Scotland) his second cousin* Mary, the daughter of George Jameson and widow of John Burnet, of Elrick, merchant and bailie in Aberdeen, by whom she had been left a widow of twenty-three years of age with two sons. George Jameson, Mrs. Gregorie's father, was an artist of great repute and has been termed the "Vandyke of Scotland." He had been a fellow pupil with Vandyke in the studio of Rubens at Antwerp.

In 1670, James Gregorie was elected Professor of Mathematics at St. Andrews. The following letter, written in the spring of 1670-1 to Mr. Collins, is preserved in the *Biographia Britannica* and refers to this period of his life:—"I am now much taken up and have been all this winter past with my public lectures, which I have twice a week, and in resolving doubts which some gentlemen and scholars propose to me. This I must comply with, nevertheless that I am often troubled with great impertinences, all persons here being ignorant of those things to admiration, so that I have but little time to spare in those studies my genius leads me to." "From which," says Sir A. Grant, "we learn that two lectures a week was the amount of teaching expected from a professor in those days, and also that a professor was regarded as a sort of oracle *pro bono publico*."

In 1673, the University of St. Andrew's commissioned Professor James Gregorie to proceed to London and there purchase instruments for mathematical and scientific purposes. But it appears that, notwithstanding this step, his scientific teaching was not approved by the St. Andrew's authorities, who did all they could to discourage him, and even kept back his salary. Hence the Professor was glad to accept the invitation which was soon proffered to the Mathematical Chair at Edinburgh, where, to use his own words, his "salary was double and his encouragements much greater."†

In 1674 the Town Council of Edinburgh took what Sir A. Grant ‡ calls "the enlightened step" of inducing James Gregorie to accept the Professorship of Mathematics at Edinburgh. Sir

---

* See "Anderson Pedigree." † See *Scots Magazine* for 1810, pp. 581-6. ‡ *Hist. Univ. Edin.*

A. Grant states that at this time, "Scotland had relapsed into a dark age of its own; but the revival of intellect was at hand, and a streak of dawn might have been observed in 1674, when the first of a family of geniuses was introduced into the College of Edinburgh." Previously, there had been no regular professors of mathematics in the university, although the title seems to have been enjoyed or assumed by one or two teachers of the subject, and practically James Gregorie became the first substantive Professor of Mathematics, and also the first non-theological professor in the college who was not hampered with the drudgery of regenting or taking classes of students through their entire course of teaching. "By the election of James Gregorie, the Council," according to Sir A. Grant, "conferred distinction upon the College, for they secured the services of a great mathematical genius, perhaps in that age second to Newton alone."

In November 1674 he delivered his inaugural address before a distinguished audience; but the hopes which were then formed were doomed to disappointment, for, in less than a year afterwards, James Gregorie's "brief and brilliant career" was brought to a close at the early age of thirty-six.

He was engaged one evening in October 1675 in showing the satellites of Jupiter to some of his pupils when he was seized with sudden and total blindness (*gutta serena*, "from a cold in the head"), and in a few days he died of a fever.

James Gregorie's "acute and penetrating genius"[*] must be allowed, and his strong originality and power of invention. At the same time he failed in lucidity and simplicity of method, qualities in which he was probably excelled by his less inventive nephew, David.

Besides the contribution to science already mentioned, James Gregorie invented a burning-glass, and there was a current report after his death that he had left behind him very considerable discoveries on the subject of infinite series in advance of the point then reached by Newton, but no papers of this description were in fact found.

---

[*] *Encyclopædia Britannica.*

A statement seems to have gained currency that in 1671 the French academicians desired to recommend James Gregorie to Louis XIV. for one of the pensions which that sovereign proposed to confer on eminent foreigners, and communications on the subject were apparently addressed to the Royal Society. James Gregorie did not take these proceedings (even if correctly stated) as more than of a complimentary nature, and he expresses himself as well contented with his circumstances, far removed as they probably were from affluence.

"His temper appears to have been warm, as appears from the conduct of his dispute with Huygens; and conscious, perhaps, of his own merits as a discoverer, he seems to have been jealous of losing any portion of this reputation by the improvement of others upon his inventions."[*]

A small tract[†] published by him (Glasgow, 1672) shows him to have possessed some sense of humour, although the wit of the tract itself is broadly ridiculed by Professor de Morgan.[‡] This publication was called *The Great Art of Weighing Vanity*, and is a satire upon Sinclair, Professor of Natural Philosophy at St. Andrew's and author of a treatise on hydrostatics. It was published under the name of Patrick Mathers, Archbeadle of the University of St. Andrew's. The authorship was for a long time attributed to James Gregorie on the authority of a note made by R. Gray, M.D., in his copy, and it has been confirmed by a letter in the *Macclesfield Correspondence* from James Gregorie to Collins.

Mr. Gregorie had one son and three daughters :—

1. Helen, born 5th December 1670, married April 1691 to Alexander Thomson, of Portlethen, Town Clerk of Aberdeen, by whom she had issue. She died 11th September 1711.
2. James, of whom below.
3. Janet, born January 1675, married to William Forbes, son of the Laird of Watertown, who first practised as

---

[*] *Encyclopædia Britannica.*
[†] This tract, with the other works of James Gregorie, was reprinted in *Scriptores Optici*, by Mr. Babbage; London, 1823. *See* De Morgan's *Budget of Paradoxes*, 124.
[‡] *Paradoxes.*

a surgeon and apothecary in Aberdeen, but was afterwards successively minister of Lesley and Tarves, at which last-mentioned place both husband and wife died. One of their children, James, was a physician in Aberdeen, and another, Thomas, is styled "an excellent mathematician."[*]

4. Isabel, who lived but a few hours.

A pension of £40 (Scots) per annum was granted by Charles II. to James, Helen and Janet Gregorie, surviving children of Professor James Gregorie, in recognition of their father's services to science.

---

[*] Old Family History.

CHAPTER IV.

THE OXFORD BRANCH.

WE now return to the elder branch of the family, the descendants of David Gregorie of Kinairdy.

IX. David Gregory, M.A., M.D., F.R.S., born 1661, died 1708.

David Gregorie, eldest son of David of Kinairdy, was born at Aberdeen, 3rd June 1659,* and received the earlier part of his education at the Marischal College there. He was sent to complete his education at Edinburgh, where his uncle, "the illustrious James,"† had recently died as the first Mathematical Professor in the University. After the death of James Gregorie a "Mr. John Young, student," appears to have acted as Mathematical Tutor without the rank of Professor, but in October 1683, upon David Gregorie passing his examination for the M.A. degree, but before he had actually received that degree, he was appointed Professor of Mathematics, with a salary of £1,000 (Scots). He was then twenty-two years of age. In December he delivered an inaugural address, "*De analyseos Geometricæ progressu et incrementis*," which, unfortunately, has not been preserved.

A MS. volume of notes of David Gregorie's course of lectures taken by Francis Pringle (afterwards Professor of Greek at St. Andrews) is preserved in the Edinburgh University Library. "The range of subjects indicated by these notes," said Professor Chrystal in 1879,‡ " will bear comparison with our curriculum as it is now. There are lectures on trigonometry, logarithms, practical geometry, geodesy, dynamics, and mechanics."

David Gregorie has been styled (by Dr. Smith) "*subtilissimi ingenii mathematicus*"; and, as will be seen, his powers were, no

---

* According to the *Shire Records of Aberdeen*, II. 189, he was born on 21st June 1661, in a house without the Port (or gate), which was then Kinairdy's, and afterwards belonged to William Walker, dyer.

† Sir A. Grant.

‡ Cited in *Story of the University of Edinburgh*.

doubt, very great, but his natural originality and aptitude for the subject were decidedly less than those of his uncle James. The possession of his uncle's papers, for whom he became a sort of literary executor, acted as a stimulus in the direction of astronomical inquiry; but his bent seems to have been towards pure mathematics rather than physical science. At Oxford, although he was Professor of Astronomy, it is said that he was hardly ever seen in the observatory.

His great claim to high rank as a scientific man rests upon his prompt acceptance and steady support of the new scientific doctrines propounded by Newton. He was the first professor to give lectures upon the Newtonian philosophy, and his classes in Edinburgh were initiated into the mysteries of the new discoveries while they were still a sealed book to the students at Cambridge.*

In 1684, Professor David Gregorie produced his first work, styled *Exercitatio Geometrica de Dimensione Figurarum, sive specimen Methodi Generalis dimetiendi quasvis Figuras:* Edinburgh, 1684, which contained some posthumous papers of his uncle's with additions of his own.

This was the only work produced by David Gregorie at Edinburgh, and it does not seem to have attracted very great attention.

A curious anecdote relating to Professor David Gregorie is preserved in Fountainhall's *Decisions of the Lords of Session*, I. 452, under date 17th March 1687:—"Captain Scot, in the King's Life Guard, having lost his dog in the College of Edinburgh, beat Mr. Gregory, Professor of Mathematics, by mistake thinking he had taken his dog. The University in a body having complained to the Lord Livingstone, Captain, and the Chancellor, of this as an affront done to them, he was secured and put to crave pardon."

David Gregorie had inherited from his mother, if not from his father, the doctrines of the Episcopal Church, and his consistent adherence to them exposed him to the hostility of the dominant

---

* Whiston's *Memoirs* of his own Life.

Presbyterian party at Edinburgh, where he was the only really distinguished man amongst the Episcopalian Professors.* The regular persecution established by the Presbyterians in 1690 rendered Mr. Gregorie ready to avail himself of the opportunity of removing to a more congenial sphere of labour, which offered itself on the resignation by Dr. Barnard, in 1691, of the Savilian Professorship of Astronomy at Oxford.

Proceeding to London with a view to his candidature for the vacant professorship, David Gregorie was fortunate enough to obtain the support and recommendation of Newton and of the Astronomer Royal, Flamsteed, and thus to secure his acceptance by the electors on 6th February 1691-2, against the strong claims of his competitor, Dr. Halley. It is satisfactory to find that notwithstanding this rivalry, Dr. Halley and David Gregorie became fast friends, and more particularly after Dr. Halley had become David Gregorie's colleague as Savilian Professor of Geometry.

The following testimonial was given in favor of Mr. David Gregorie by Sir Isaac Newton, dated London, July 1691:

> "Being desired by Mr. David Gregorie, Mathematic Professor of the Colledge in Edinburgh to testifie my knowledge of him, and having known him by his printed mathematical performances, and by discoursing with travellers from Scotland, and of late by conversing with him, I do account him one of the most able and judicious mathematicians of his age now living. He is very well skilled in analysis and geometry both new and old. He has been conversant in the best writers about astronomy and understands that science very well. He is not only acquainted with books but his invention in mathematical things is also good. He has performed his duty at Edinburgh with credit, as I hear, and advanced the mathematicks. He is reputed the greatest mathematician in Scotland, and that deservedly, so far as my knowledge reaches, for I esteem him an ornament to his country, and upon these accounts do recommend him to the duties of the Astronomy Professor into the place in Oxford now vacant.—Sic subscribitur,
> "Is. NEWTON, Math. Prof. Cantab."†

On his first arrival in London, Mr. Gregorie was elected a Fellow of the Royal Society, and thenceforward was a constant contributor to the *Philosophical Transactions*.

---

* Burton's *Hist. Scot.* I. 223.   † Nichols' *Illustrations of Literature*, IV. 49.

In order to qualify himself for his professorship, David Gregorie (or Gregory as he seems now to have called himself) entered at Balliol, and forthwith was granted the degrees of M.A. and M.D. by incorporation.

In 1693 he communicated to the *Philosophical Transactions* a resolution of the Florentine problem *De Testudine veliformi quadribili*, and in 1695 he published at Oxford a more important work containing the substance of some of his Edinburgh lectures of eleven years before.

Of this work, which was entitled *Catoptricæ et Dioptricæ Sphericæ Elementa*, Dr. Keill* made the extravagantly complimentary prediction that it would last as long as the sun or moon! It was afterwards republished first with additions by Dr. William Brown, and with the recommendation of Mr. Jones and Dr. Desaguliers, and afterwards in 1735 by Dr. Desaguliers himself, accompanied with an account of the Gregorian and Newtonian telescopes. In this treatise Dr. David Gregory made an observation which showed that what is generally believed to have been a discovery of much later date—the construction of achromatic telescopes—had suggested itself to him from a consideration of the mode in which achromatism is effected in the human eye by means of the conjunction of the different humours.

In 1697, Dr. David Gregory published in the *Philosophical Transactions* a full demonstration—the first ever given—of the numerous properties of the "catenary," or curve in which a chain (Latin, *catena*) naturally hangs. This paper (which is dedicated to Dean Aldrich, of Christ Church) was republished in 1706 in the *Miscellanea Curiosa* as being one of the "noblest discoveries" that had ever been presented to the Royal Society.

The value of these investigations will be at once perceived by anyone who has a knowledge of mechanics.

In 1702, David Gregory produced at Oxford his most important treatise, *Astronomiæ Physicæ et Geometricæ Elementa*. In this were included several propositions communicated by Newton,† being

---
* *Quarterly Review*, LXXXIV., 309.
† The MSS. of Newton here referred to were, with other MSS. belonging to James and David Gregory, presented by the late John Gregory (Advocate) to the Royal Society of London.

results which their author had not obtained at the time of the publication of the first edition of the *Principia*, but was anxious to bring before the public at once without waiting for the second edition of his own work. Dr. Gregory's book also contained a very complete history of the science of astronomy from the earliest times.

After Dr. Gregory's death it was translated into English (1726) by Edmund Stone, F.R.S.

In 1703, Dr. Gregory published an edition of Euclid in Greek and Latin in prosecution of the design formed by his predecessor, Dr. Barnard, of producing editions of all the ancient mathematicians. In this task he was assisted by Hudson, and the work was dedicated to Dean Aldrich.* In furtherance of the same plan, Dr. Gregory, in conjunction with Dr. Halley, undertook an edition of the *Conics* of Apollonius, which had been edited a century before by Professor Anderson of Paris, *supra* p. 12. He did not live to see the completion of this work. On 10th October 1708 Dr. Gregory died at Maidenhead in Berkshire on his journey from London to Bath for his health. He was buried at Maidenhead, but his widow erected a monument to his memory in Great St. Mary's Church, Oxford, on one of the north-west pillars of the nave.†

Amongst other unfinished works Dr. David Gregory left, in manuscript, *A Short Treatise on the Nature and Arithmetic of Logarithms*, which is printed at the end of Dr. Keith's translation of Commandine's *Euclid*, and a *Treatise on Practical Geometry*, which was afterwards translated and published in 1745 by Maclaurin, a second edition being issued in 1751. This work, according to Sir A. Grant, was regularly used in the last century as a university text-book.

Other unfinished works were Treatises on *Fluxions*, *Mechanics* and *Hydrostatics*.

"To the genius and ability of Dr. David Gregory," says Sir A. Grant, "the most celebrated mathematicians of the age, Sir Isaac Newton, Halley, and Keill, gave ample testimonies." Indeed, it

---

* Wood's *Antiquities of Oxford* and Hearne's MSS. Collection, V., 178, 181.
† See inscription, also letters from Dr. Arbuthnot to Dr. Chaslett on his death.

appears that he enjoyed, in a high degree, the confidence and friendship of Sir Isaac Newton who entrusted him with a MS. copy of his *Principia* with a view to his making observations thereon. Of these observations—which appear to be interesting, and having been made too late for the first edition of the *Principia*, were made use of in the second—a complete copy is preserved in the library of the University of Edinburgh. Besides the testimonial above set out, Newton's opinion of David Gregory is recorded in a letter to Flamsteed, in which, referring to their common scientific work, he says, "If you and I live not long enough, Mr. Gregory and Mr. Halley are both young men."

It was apparently at one time contemplated to appoint Dr. David Gregory tutor to the young Duke of Gloucester, son of Queen Anne; Dr. Burnet, Bishop of Salisbury (a friend, as we have seen, of James Gregorie) having at the time paramount influence at Court and a genuine desire to push his countrymen into prominent situations.*

Dr. David married 14th July 1695 Elizabeth, daughter of Mr. Charles Oliphant, of Langton, in Scotland, and by her had nine children:—

1. David, born at Oxford 14th July 1696, of whom below, p. 36.
2. Elizabeth, born at Oxford 29th December 1697, died 1st October 1700.
3. John, born at Oxford 23rd September 1699, died 25th March 1701.
4. James, born at Oxford 15th April 1701.
5. Barbara, born at Oxford 9th July 1702, died of small-pox in London October 1708.
6. Thomas, born at Oxford 23rd December 1703, died 12th January 1704.
7. Charles, born at London 13th April 1705, admitted scholar of Westminster 1720, died 1724.
8. Isaac, so named after Newton, born in London 7th December 1706.
9. Philip, born in London 11th January 1708.

* Nichols.

It has been stated above * that, in 1690, David Gregorie of Kinairdy made over the Kinairdy property to Dr. David Gregory. It appears also from the *Statistical Account of Scotland* that, in 1702, Dr. David, with the consent of his wife, sold the property to Mr. Thomas Donaldson, from whom it passed into the hands of the Earl of Fife's family, with whom it still remains.

X. David Gregory, D.D., born 1696, died 1767.

David Gregory, eldest son of the Savilian professor, is frequently mentioned in Wood's *Antiquities of Oxford*, and a notice of him is to be found in the *Alumni Westmonasterienses*. In 1714 he was elected a student of Christ Church, Oxford, from Westminster School, of which he was a scholar. After graduating at Oxford he became rector of Semly, Wilts, and, in 1723, was appointed Professor of Modern History (with which modern languages were then associated), in the University of Oxford, on the foundation of that professorship by George I. He took the degree of B.D. 13th March 1731, and D.D. 7th July 1732. Dr. Gregory was appointed canon of Christ Church 8th June 1736, and thereupon resigned his professorship. As canon, he superintended the restoration of the Hall (to which he presented the busts of George I. and George II.), and the enlargement of the library of Christ Church.

On the 18th May 1756, Dr. Gregory was appointed Dean of Christ Church, and afterwards Prolocutor of the Lower House of Convocation, and later Master of Sherborne Hospital near Durham. During his mastership great improvements were made in the accommodation for the poor brethren.

There are no literary remains of Dean Gregory, except some Latin hexameters, printed among the Academical Verses, upon the death of George I. and the accession of George II., and another Latin poem written in 1761 on the death of the latter monarch and the accession of his grandson.

---

* Page 18.

Dean Gregory married Lady Mary Grey, youngest daughter of Henry Grey, Duke of Kent (whose title died with him), and by her had issue as follows:—

1. David, who died in the East Indies unmarried.
2. George, for a time student at Christ Church, married and died s.p. at Dumfries 16th November 1785, and was buried there.
3. Henry, educated at Westminster. He was killed by a fall from his horse at Newmarket, s.p. and under age, April 1773.
4. Jemima, died unmarried in London 19th January 1793.
5. Mary, died 7th January 1745.
6. James, died 22nd March 1750.

Dean Gregory died in 1767 in his 71st year, and was buried in Christ Church Cathedral in the same grave as his wife, who died in 1762. By his will the Dean made a curious and ill-worded disposition of his valuable library, apparently intending that if his sons George and Henry, or one of them, did not take up some literary calling, the library should pass to Dr. James Gregory of Edinburgh.* These two young men seem to have run most unsatisfactory careers, and one of them at least became insolvent; but upon the wording of the will no claim to the books appeared capable of being effectually set up by Dr. James Gregory, and in the result, as the Dean's sons and their creditors were either unwilling or unable to take possession of them, the books remained in the custody of Christ Church, Oxford, where, it is to be hoped, they now remain as a highly esteemed part of the Library of the Foundation.

This branch of the family is now extinct.

* Post, page 60.

CHAPTER V.

THE AMERICAN BRANCH.

THE elder line being now shewn to be extinct we return to

IX. James Gregorie, the fifth son of David of Kinairdy, born 1666, died 1742.

James Gregorie was born 29th April 1666, and graduated at Edinburgh in May 1685.* He was shortly afterwards appointed to the Chair of Moral Philosophy at St. Andrews, but resigned it at the Restoration. In 1692 he succeeded his elder brother David as Professor of Mathematics in the University of Edinburgh, on the removal of the latter to Oxford; but as the College revenues were low at the time, James Gregorie had to accept the chair on a diminished salary of 900 merks, or £50 sterling, in addition to the student's fees.† There is a notice of him in the *Encyclopædia Britannica*, in which he is called "an eminent mathematician," and Sir A. Grant † says of him that he was "an able teacher," but that he did not "otherwise add to the reputation of the Gregory Family." In 1690 he published a "*Compendium of Newton's Philosophy*," and in 1701 he obtained a patent for a machine for raising water "merely by lifting, without suction or forcing." On his retirement, owing to age and infirmity, in 1725, Colin Maclaurin was made joint Professor with him, with right of succession, Sir Isaac Newton offering to contribute during his life £20 a-year towards making a provision for him "till Mr. Gregorie's place became void." Mr. Gregorie, however, managed to live on for 17 years, during which Maclaurin got no salary.†

Professor James Gregorie married, 4th September 1698, Barbara, daughter of Charles Oliphant, of Langton, then deceased, and sister

---

* *Book of Edinburgh Graduates*, Ballantyne Society.
† *Story of the University of Edinburgh*.

of his brother David's wife, and by her (who died in 1714) he had
three sons and five daughters,* viz. :—

1. Barbara, born 13th October 1699.
2. Elizabeth, baptised 9th November 1700.
3. James.
4. William, of whom below.
5. Charles, born 17th February 1709.
6. Christian, who survived her father.
7. Daughter.
8. Daughter.†

X. William Gregory emigrated to Massachusetts, and died
there in 1740. He married a daughter of Mr. James Walker, of
Walpole, Mass., and had issue two sons,‡ viz. :—

1. John, who was killed by an accident;
2. William, born 1731, see below;

and four daughters, who married husbands of the respective names
of Harrington, Whitmore, Morse and Upham.

XI. William Gregory was born at Walpole, Mass., 19th July
1731, and died in 1824. He married Experience Robbins, who died
in 1827, and by her he had twelve children :—

1. Elizabeth.
2. William, who died in 1757.
3. Experience, who died in 1758.
4. Experience.

---

* The family history of Dr. James Gregorie gives only two sons and five daughters, while a later history gives three sons. Neither mentions the name of any son except James. A search, by the writer, of the Register of the city of Edinburgh over the period of Professor James Gregorie's married life resulted in the discovery of the entries of baptism of Barbara, Elizabeth and Charles only. A letter, however, is extant in the possession of Mr. Silas W. Gregory, of San Francisco, written by an amanuensis on behalf of James Gregorie, from Edinburgh, to Mr. Walker, of Walpole, Mass., acknowledging the receipt of the news of the death of James Gregorie's son William. The letter is dated 8th August 1741. The identity of the James Gregorie in question with the above professor is proved by the seal on the letter (see Supplemental Chapter). The connection between Mr. Silas Gregory's family and that which is the subject of these records has always been a tradition in the former family, but between 1741 and 1884 no communication passed between the American branch and any other members of the family.

† One of the daughters was the subject of David Mallet's poem "William and Margaret."

‡ This and the remaining information as to this branch is given by Mr. H. P. Gregory.

5. William.
6. Frances, who died in 1773.
7. Mary.
8. John, born 1769, died 1868 (married).
9. Josiah, of whom below.
10. Olive.
11. Luther, who died in 1779.
12. Luther.

XII. Josiah Gregory, born 1771, died 1870. He married Meletiah Payson (born 1767, died 1830), and by her had eight children, viz. :—

1. Noyes Payson, of whom below.
2. Amos, born 1793.
3. Charity, born 1794.
4. Wealthy, born 1796.
5. Meletiah, born 1798.
6. Josiah, born 1799.
7. Sarah, born 1802.
8. Mary, born 1806.

XIII. Noyes Payson Gregory, born 1791, died 1876. He married first Lucy Hunter, and by her had five daughters, viz. :—

1. Mary, married to Robert Smith, died 1883.
2. Louisa, married to Hiram Haile.
3. Lucy E., married to R. G. Stone, died 1869.*
4. Wealthy, married to Albert Marshall, died 1860.
5. Lucretia, married to John Hutchinson.

Mr. N. P. Gregory afterwards married (secondly) Henrietta Hunter, and by her had two children, viz. :—

1. Silas Wright, who married Grace Hopkins, and has five children :—Annie, Louise, Margherite, Grace and Donald McGregor.
2. Henry Payson Gregory, who married Elise Stewart McClure, and has three children :—David McClure, Elise and Kenneth.

* She had issue five daughters, viz.: Anna, Harriette, Lucy, Frances, and Katherine.

CHAPTER VI.
THE ST. ANDREW'S BRANCH.

WE now return to the fourth son of David Gregorie of Kinairdy by his second marriage, viz. :—

IX. Charles Gregorie, born 14th February 1681, died about 1739.

Charles Gregorie is also the subject of a short notice in the *Encyclopædia Britannica*. In 1707 he was created Professor of Mathematics at St. Andrews by Queen Anne, and held his chair for 32 years "with reputation and ability." About 1739 he resigned in favour of his son David. He married Margaret Campbell, and by her had three children :—

1. Margaret, baptised 21st December 1710.
2. David, baptised 19th September 1712.
3. Isabel, baptised 29th January 1714.

X. David Gregorie, born 1712, died 1765.

David Gregorie was for some time tutor to the sons of the Duke of Gordon, with whom his grandmother was connected.* In 1739 he succeeded his father as Professor of Mathematics at St. Andrews. He is described in the *Encyclopædia Britannica* as having "eminently inherited the talents of his family," and his cousin, Professor Reid, speaks of him as "a well-bred, sensible gentleman, and much esteemed as a laborious and excellent teacher." He published only one work, viz., a *Compendium of Algebra*, which was "an excellent text-book."† His zeal for the kirk is referred to in the *Quarterly Review*, I., 376. He appears to have come into collision with Mr. Stockdale, a student, in 1756 over the latter's irregularity in attendance at kirk. He married Miss Paterson, by whom he had a son Charles, and a daughter Catherine. The latter married Captain John Graham-Bonar, of Greigston, Fifeshire, by whom she had issue.

Professor David Gregorie died in 1765.

XI. Charles Gregorie, born 1751, died   .

Charles Gregorie, born 22nd November 1751, entered the service of the East India Company, and was captain of an

---

* See p. 20 *infra*.   † So says Dr. Reid.

Indiaman, called the "*Fortitude*." He married, 7th June 1787, Catherine Sophia, only child of George Macaulay, M.D.,* of London, by his second wife Catherine Sawbridge,† a lady who acquired a considerable literary reputation. By that lady (who died suddenly 8th April 1821) Captain Gregorie had four children :—

1. Catherine, born 19th August 1788, died 18th December 1870, was married to John Fortescue Brickdale, Esq., in July 1813, by whom she had issue.
2. David William, of whom below.
3. Charles, born 14th April 1791, Captain in the 13th Light Dragoons. He served through the Peninsular War and at Waterloo, and afterwards sold out of the Army. He died on 16th October 1858 unmarried.
4. George, born 21st November 1792, M.A. Christ Church, Oxford, Barrister-at-law, died unmarried.

XII. David William Gregorie, born 25th April 1790, died 15th October 1842.

David William Gregorie was M.A. of Christ Church, Oxon, and a Barrister of Lincoln's Inn. In 1825 he was appointed one of the Police Magistrates of London, and sat in the Westminster Police Court. He married Eleanor St. Barbe White, and by her had four children, viz. :—

1. Charles Frederick, Colonel in the Army, C.B., married Henrietta Amy Lawrence. He has a son, David George, Lieutenant 18th Royal Irish Fusiliers, and other issue, as shewn in the pedigree.
2. George Wayne, married Eliza Sarah Harwood, and has issue as shewn in the pedigree.
3. Eleanor Mary, died 24th February 1856.
4. Catherine Blanche.

* He was son of Archibald Macaulay, Lord Provost of Edinburgh. His sister Anne married David Gregorie, of Dunkirk (*see* next page); another sister (Jane) married Fraser, of Balnain, and her eldest daughter (Anne) married Tytler, of Woodhouselee, and carried the Fraser property into that family. Catherine, second daughter of Jane Fraser, married another David Gregorie, of Dunkirk (*see* page 44 *infra*).

† Mrs. Macaulay, daughter of John Sawbridge, of Ollantigh, Kent, born 1730, married Dr. Macaulay in 1760. After his death she married (1778) a clergyman named Graham. She afterwards went to America, became intimate with Washington, and wrote several historical works of a republican tendency, including a History of England (in 8 vols.) from James I. to the Accession of the House of Hanover; she died in 1791.

CHAPTER VII.

THE DUNKIRK BRANCH.

THE next branch of the family is that descended from George Gregorie, sixth son of the second marriage of David Gregorie, of Kinairdy. Of this branch we have very slight records. It may be stated by way of preface that there was in the 17th century, and until the middle of the 18th, a trading colony or factory of Scotsmen at Campvere, in the province of Zealand, in Holland, which enjoyed peculiar privileges. The colony was presided over by a high official of State, called the Lord Conservator of Scots Privileges at Campvere, a dignity which survived, as a sinecure, until late in the last century, after the privileges themselves had been abolished.

IX. George Gregorie, born 1685, died 1731, was a "staple-factor" at Campvere, and although at one time he took to the study of mathematics, he found it interfered with his business, and he accordingly dropped his scientific pursuits. He married Sophia Van Wyngarden, a well-connected Dutch lady (said to have been related to the Prince of Orange), who survived him, and afterwards married David Gregorie, son of Dr. James Gregorie, of Aberdeen, as mentioned below.* He had two sons:—
   1. David, of whom below.
   2. John, who resided at Campvere, and had two children, Leonard and Sophia.

X. David Gregorie was born in the Scots factory at Campvere, and succeeded his step-father as one of the staple-factors there in 1739. He afterwards moved to Dunkirk, where he continued to carry on business. He was married twice, viz., first to Anne Macaulay, youngest daughter of Archibald Macaulay, Lord Provost of Edinburgh; and secondly to another Scotch lady. The former

---
* Page 46.

Mrs. Gregorie died in giving birth to her first child. David Gregorie had in all three sons, viz. :—

1. George, born at Dunkirk 1st August 1758, died in 1822, leaving a son.
2. David, merchant at Dunkirk, and afterwards at St. Omer, died in 1822. He married Catherine Fraser, daughter of the Laird of Balnain, in Invernesshire, and niece of his father's first wife, by which lady he had a son, David, who was in the French Army, and fell in battle, and three daughters, viz., Emily, wife of Colonel Vannechent; Catherine, who married a Frenchman; and Caroline.
3. John, born in 1761 at Dunkirk, where he resided for some time. In or about 1826 he also moved to St. Omer with his daughters, he and the young son of his eldest brother George being then the only male representatives of their branch of the family.

Since 1826 no communication has passed between the Dunkirk branch and any other members of the family.

CHAPTER VIII.

THE ABERDEEN AND EDINBURGH BRANCH.

HAVING now, so far as existing information will allow, traced the descendants of David Gregorie, of Kinairdy, we return to the family of his younger brother, Professor James Gregorie, who, as we have seen, left an only son, James.

IX. James Gregorie, M.D., born 1674, died 1733.

James Gregorie,* who was born at St. Andrews 4th February 1674, and educated at the Schools of Aberdeen and Universities of Aberdeen and Edinburgh, applied himself to the study of medicine. In 1696 he went to Holland, where the hostilities between William III. and Louis XIV., which had broken out immediately after the former's accession to the English Throne, were still continuing. Mr. Gregorie spent the summer with the English Army in Flanders, and upon the conclusion of the Treaty of Ryswick in September 1697 went to Utrecht and afterwards to Paris. In September 1698 he returned to Holland, visiting the French camp *en route*, and obtaining in that month the degree of M.D. at Rheims. Shortly afterwards he returned to London, and after a brief stay there proceeded to Chelmsford, in Essex, with a view to commencing the practice of his profession. His stay at Chelmsford was, however, of short duration, and in November 1699 he returned to his native country and settled in Aberdeen as a physician.†

On 23rd December 1725 Dr. James Gregorie was unanimously elected Professor of Medicine (or " Mediciner ") in King's College,

---

* There are notices of him in the *Book of Bon Accord* and in the *Encyclopædia Britannica*.

† At this period there were of course in Aberdeen no persons practising as what are now called "general practitioners." The professions of physicians and surgeons were completely dissociated, the surgeons being held of a lower order, and included with the "litsters" and barbers in one of the "trade corporations" of the city (*see* above, p. 12). A few surgeons kept apothecaries' shops for retail trade, but, as there were no regular apothecaries, the physicians were obliged to keep and compound at their own houses medicines for the use of their patients alone, but they did not, of course, sell their drugs to the general public.

Aberdeen, and beheld that office until his resignation on 20th December 1732, when his son James was elected in his place.

Dr. Gregorie is commonly considered the founder of the Medical School at Aberdeen, and is spoken of as "a man of strong, sound, practical sense." He was long remembered as the author of many local improvements, including the planting of the 'Mediciner's Glebe.' He constructed a stone rampart at the mouth of the River Don with a view to protecting the bed of the river and improving the Salmon Fisheries; and, in return for these services, the proprietors of the Fisheries granted to him "a half net's fishing" in the river. The rampart, which as late as 1826 bore the name of "Dr. Gregorie's Dyke," is still in existence, and the fishings granted, as just mentioned, remained in the elder branch of Dr. Gregorie's descendants until—under the will of Georgina Gregory, who died in 1877—they devolved (on the death of Henry John Makdougall Gregory, under age) upon Mrs. Leith, a descendant of Dr. James Gregorie's grand-daughter Anna Forbes. Dr. Gregorie married, 4th November 1702, Catherine, second daughter of Sir John Forbes, of Monymusk (3rd Baronet), by his second wife Barbara, daughter of Dalmahoy of that ilk. Mrs. Gregorie died of consumption 25th July 1715, aged 32, having had issue:

1. James, born 8th June 1704, died of small-pox 22nd May 1705.
2. John, born 14th January 1706, died also of small-pox 6th May 1711.
3. James, born 3rd December 1707, of whom below, next page.
4. Barbara, born 18th June 1709, died also of small-pox 14th May 1711.
5. David, born 7th October 1711. He served an apprenticeship to his cousin George Gregorie, already mentioned as staple-factor at Campvere, and succeeded him in that capacity. He married his cousin's widow Sophia Van Wyngarden, and died in 1739, leaving one young child Katherine.
6. John, born 27th March 1713, died of small-pox 30th July 1714.

Dr. James Gregorie married, secondly, 22nd June 1719, Anna, only child of Principal George Chalmers,* of King's College, Aberdeen, by his marriage with Christian Campbell, daughter of Mr. George Campbell, Professor of Divinity in Edinburgh.†

Mrs. Gregorie (née Chalmers) died suddenly in 1770 while sitting at table. She was a victim to gout, which became hereditary in her descendants.

Dr. James Gregorie had issue by his second marriage:

1. George, born 15th September 1720, died of consumption at Amiens, in France, about 1741, whilst prosecuting the study of medicine, unmarried. His brother Dr. John appears to have held the highest opinion of his abilities and promise.
2. Christian, born 12th April 1722, died of small-pox 1725.
3. John, of whom below, next page.

Dr. James Gregorie died in January 1733.

X. James Gregorie, M.D., born 1707, died 1755.‡

James Gregorie was born 3rd December 1707, and graduated M.D. at Aberdeen in 1728. He succeeded his father as Professor of Medicine in King's College, Aberdeen, 20th December 1732. He married Helen,§ daughter of Andrew Burnet, of Elrick, but had no issue.

This Dr. James Gregorie, in the year 1715, had a narrow escape (as related by Sir Walter Scott in his preface to *Rob Roy*) of being carried off by his relative Rob Roy,‖ and, as the latter expressed it, of being "made a man of" according to Highland ideas. In

---

* *See* above, p. 20. Probably the great-grand-daughter of David Gregorie of Kinairdy, there mentioned as having married Principal Chalmers, was his second wife.

† Dr. Carlyle, in his autobiography mentioned below (page 49), states (p. 223): "There was an assistant preacher at Inveresk, George Anderson, son of a clergyman in Fife, and, by his mother, grandson of a Professor Campbell, of Edinburgh, who made a figure in the Divinity Chair towards the end of the seventeenth century. His aunt was the mother of Dr. John Gregory, of Edinburgh, but he had not partaken of the smallest spark of genius from either of the families."

‡ He is mentioned in the *Book of Bon Accord*.

§ This lady was his cousin by the half-blood (*see* Anderson Pedigree), she survived her husband (*see* page 52).

‖ Rob Roy was descended from a younger brother of Gregor Macgregor (No. I above p. 9).

the insurrection of that year Rob Roy had occupied Aberdeen with a force of the rebels, and he offered for young James Gregorie the ultimate prospect of becoming lieutenant of his clan, an offer which, under the circumstances, his father had some difficulty in refusing. Sir Walter Scott says that Dr. James, "like most of his family," was distinguished for his scientific acquirements. "He was rather of an irritable and pertinacious disposition, and his friends were wont to remark when he showed any symptom of these foibles, 'Ah! this comes of not having been educated by Rob Roy.'" "These details," says Sir Walter Scott, "which bring the highest pitch of civilization so closely into contact with the half-savage state of society, I have heard told by the late distinguished Dr. James Gregory."*

Dr. James Gregorie suffered from periodical attacks of illness, to one of which he succumbed, on 18th November 1755.

X. John Gregory, M.D., F.R.S., F.R.C.P., born 1724, died 1773.†

John Gregory, the youngest son of Dr. James Gregorie (No. IX.), born at Aberdeen, 3rd June 1724, is the member of the family who has most distinguished himself in literature. A complete collection of his works in four volumes was published after his death by his son Dr. James Gregory, prefixed to which was an account of his life, and a memoir of his ancestors, written by his intimate friend Alexander Fraser-Tytler (Lord Woodhouselee).

There is a notice of him in *Davenport's Dictionary of Biography*, and a life of him was also published by the naturalist Dr. Smellie. An account of him in the *Encyclopædia Britannica* appears to have been from the pen of, or to have been revised by, Dr. James Gregory, and to have been taken chiefly from Lord Woodhouselee's life.

The *European Magazine and London Review* for June 1806 contains an account of Dr. John Gregory, almost identical with that in the *Encyclopædia Britannica*, together with a portrait.

---

* No. XI., *post*, p. 60.

† Dr. John Gregory and his descendants dropped the "ie" termination. See p. 1.

By reason of the death of his father, when John Gregory was only in the ninth year of his age, the direction of the latter's education devolved upon his grandfather, Principal Chalmers, and his elder half-brother, Dr. James Gregorie, who was already Professor of Medicine at Aberdeen; but the course of his studies was much influenced by the advice and assistance of his cousin Dr. Reid, the well-known moral philosopher.* The rudiments of his classical education he received at the Grammar School of Aberdeen, after leaving which he went through the usual curriculum at the King's College of that city.

The style of his writings bears ample testimony to his attainments as a scholar, as well as to his powers as a scientific reasoner.†

Mr. Gregory, having now decided upon following the medical profession, proceeded, in 1742, with a view to further study, and accompanied by his mother, to Edinburgh, where the School of Medicine was then rising rapidly in public estimation. In the same year he became a member of the Edinburgh Medical Society, an association which had been founded in 1737 for the free discussion of all questions connected with medicine and philosophy. Amongst his colleagues in this society was his fellow student and intimate companion Mark Akenside, the physician and poet.

After completing the medical course at Edinburgh Mr. Gregory next (in 1745) went to Leyden, then the principal Medical School of the Continent, and there studied under Gaubinus, Albinus, and Van Royen. Amongst his numerous acquaintances there were John Wilkes and Charles Townsend.

Many interesting details concerning Dr. John Gregory are to be found in the autobiography (Blackwood 1860) of Dr. Alexander Carlyle, sometime Minister of Inveresk, who was a fellow student with Dr. Gregory at Leyden. It appears (p. 165) that they, as well as Wilkes and a certain Dr. Monckly, lodged in

---

* *See* above, page 20.

† While these sheets were passing through the press there were published two interesting and well-written volumes, entitled *Eminent Doctors, their Lives and their Work*, by G. T. Bettany. The author's estimates of Dr. John Gregory and his son, Dr. James, as well as the references to the reputation of the family, are interesting as giving an independent and professional view of the subjects of these Records.

"the house of Madame Van der Tasse on the Long Bridge." Dr. Monckly had a habit of getting ideas from Dr. John Gregory, and then bringing them out in the course of general conversation with other students as his own, Dr. Gregory being "above the desire of shining," and not exposing the misappropriation. This system was sometimes carried further, and in one instance, given by Dr. Carlyle (p. 177), the offender appears to have managed the case of a patient on the strength of the private and unacknowledged advice of Dr. Gregory, claiming for himself alone the full benefit of the success achieved.

Dr. Carlyle gives his estimate of Dr. John Gregory as follows:—*

"Gregory, though a far abler man than Monckly, and not less a man of learning for his age than of taste, in the most important qualities, was not superior to Monckly. When he was afterwards tried by the ardent spirits of Edinburgh, and the prying eyes of rivalship, he did not escape without the imputation of being cold, selfish and cunning. His pretensions to be more religious than others of his profession, and his constant eulogies on the female sex as at least equal, if not superior, to the male, were supposed to be lures of reputation or professional arts to get into business.

"When those objections were made to him at Edinburgh, I was able to take off the edge from them by assuring people that his notions and modes of talking were not newly adopted for a purpose, for that when at Leyden at the age of 21 or 22 he was equally incessant and warm on those topics, though he had not a female to flatter, nor ever went to church, but when I dragged him to please old Gowan. Having found Aberdeen too narrow a circle for him, he tried London for a twelvemonth without success, for being ungainly in his person and manner, and no lucky accident having befallen him, he could not make his way suddenly in a situation where external graces and address go much further than profound learning or professional skill. Dr. Gregory, however, was not without address, for he was much a master of conversation on all subjects, and, without gross flattery, obtained even more than a favourable hearing to himself, for, not contradicting you at first, but rather assenting or yielding, as it were, to your knowledge and taste, he very often brought you round to think as he did, and to consider him a superior man. In all my dealings with him—for he was my family physician—I found him friendly, affectionate and generous."

During his stay at Leyden Dr. Gregory received a remarkable honour in the degree of M.D., which in his absence and without

* Page 460.

solicitation was granted to him by King's College, Aberdeen, 11th March 1746. Soon after this event Dr. Gregory returned to Aberdeen, and on 3rd June 1746 was elected Regent or Professor of Philosophy in the same University. In this capacity he gave lectures in 1747-8-9 on mathematics and moral and natural philosophy, while at the same time he commenced practice as a physician in Aberdeen.

In 1749 Dr. Gregory found that the duties of his Regentship interfered so much with his professional practice that on 8th September 1749 he resigned his office, being succeeded by his cousin Dr. Thomas Reid.

Shortly after this date he appears to have spent a few months on the Continent, and on his return in 1752 he married the Hon. Elizabeth Forbes, the younger of the two surviving daughters of the 13th Lord Forbes. Of this young lady (who was born 5th January 1730) Lord Woodhouselee writes,* in 1789, that " to the exterior endowments of great beauty and engaging manners, she joined a very superior understanding, and an uncommon share of wit," and that with her Dr. Gregory received "a handsome addition of fortune."† A lawsuit which arose in reference to Mrs. Gregory's portion and that of her sister Mrs. Dundas is recorded 2 *Fac. Dec.*, 203—12th Feb. 1755.

Dr. Gregory's principal literary work, *A Father's Legacy to his Daughters*, gives the reader some idea of the character and qualities of the wife whose loss was the occasion of the work itself.

The field of medical practice at Aberdeen being at this time in a great measure occupied by Dr. James Gregorie, the elder brother of Dr. John, the latter determined to try his fortune in London. Thither he accordingly went in 1754, and being (as it is said)‡ "already known there by reputation," he found an easy introduction to many persons of social and literary eminence, and, amongst others, to Sir George (afterwards Lord) Lyttelton, Chancellor of the Exchequer. The latter became a fast friend of Dr. Gregory, and in later years proved of great service to him in aiding and encouraging him in his literary enterprises.

---

* Preface to Dr. John Gregory's works. † *See* the accompanying Pedigree of Mrs. Gregory.
‡ By Lord Woodhouselee.

Dr. Gregory likewise enjoyed the friendship of Mr. Edward Montague, and more particularly of his celebrated wife Mrs. Montague, "whose drawing rooms in London then united the fashion and talent of England."*

On his arrival in London Dr. Gregory was at once elected a Fellow of the Royal Society of London, and "daily advancing in the public esteem it is not to be doubted that, had he continued his residence in that metropolis, his professional talents would have found their reward in a very extensive practice,"† but the death of his brother Dr. James Gregorie, in October 1755, occasioning a vacancy in the Professorship of Medicine in King's College, Aberdeen, which he was solicited to fill, and to which he was elected in his absence (10th May 1756), he returned to Aberdeen, and again took up the duties of a Professorial Chair. Dr. John Gregory endeavoured to found permanent medical lectures at Aberdeen, but from the paucity of students the attempt temporarily failed. ‡

The death of Dr. James involved Dr. John in legal troubles (see "Dr. Gregory v. Helen Burnet, 11th August 1757, 2 *Fac. Reports*, 86"). The Defendant was relict of Dr. James, and Dr. John was bound under a bond to infeft her in one-third of his lands of Blairtown and Hopehill to secure an annuity to her. The Doctor wishing to sell these properties offered Mrs. Gregorie, and endeavoured to compel her to accept, a substituted security on his Don Fisheries, then let at £85 per annum. This attempt, of course, failed.

On 29th November 1763 a grievous blow fell upon Dr. Gregory in the death of his wife in her confinement, and in 1764, partly with a view to relieving himself from the painful associations of Aberdeen, and partly with a view to a more extended practice, Dr. Gregory removed to Edinburgh. His University, however, did not compel him to resign his professorship entirely, the only change being that in 1765 Sir Alexander Gordon, of Lessmore, was associated with him as joint professor.

---

* Sir A. Alison.

† Lord Woodhouselee. Dr. Carlyle, it will have been seen, took a different view. Mr. Bestany, in *Eminent Doctors*, says, "Dr. Gregory would, no doubt, have obtained fashionable support."

‡ *Statistical Account of Scotland*.

In 1766 Dr. Gregory was elected Professor of the Practice of Physic in the University of Edinburgh on the resignation of Dr. Rutherford. This appointment was far from giving universal satisfaction.* Dr. Cullen, the Professor of Chemistry, was generally regarded as the appropriate successor of Dr. Rutherford, but the latter had imbibed such a strong prejudice against the former that, although desirous of retirement, he would not resign his office so long as the succession was likely to fall to the object of his aversion. The Town Council (then the governing body of Edinburgh University) were, it is said, induced by Dr. Rutherford to bring Dr. Gregory from Aberdeen, and Dr. Thomson says that though the latter was "a physician qualified in many respects to do high honor to the University, Cullen's pretensions to the Chair in question must be viewed as paramount to those of every other candidate." There seems some inaccuracy in these statements, inasmuch as it appears from Lord Woodhouselee's Life of Dr. Gregory, that the latter was settled in Edinburgh two years before his election to his professorship there.

Upon his election at Edinburgh Dr. Gregory entirely resigned his chair at Aberdeen in favour of Sir Alexander Gordon.

In the same year (1766) a vacancy occurred in two important medical posts by the death of Dr. Whytt, who was Professor of the Institutes, or Theory, of Medicine at Edinburgh, and also First Physician to the King for Scotland. Dr. Whytt's professorship was filled by the appointment of Dr. Cullen, whose disappointment on the occasion above referred to seems to have rendered him at first unwilling to accept what was apparently considered an inferior chair; while Dr. Gregory became First Physician to the King.

In 1767, 1768, and 1769 Dr. Gregory lectured on the Practice of Medicine, and afterwards he and Dr. Cullen concluded an agreement under which the two Professors gave alternate courses of the theory and practice, so that Dr. Cullen obtained by anticipation some part of the distinction which he coveted, and to the sole enjoyment of which he succeeded on Dr. Gregory's death in 1773.†

---
* See Dr Thomson's "Life and Writings of Cullen," *Edinburgh Review*, LV., 467, *Story of the University of Edinburgh*, and Bettany's *Eminent Doctors*.

† Sir A. Grant states that in 1767 the Town Council appointed the two to be joint Professors of the Theory and Practice of Medicine, but of this appointment no evidence is extant

Dr. Carlyle's account of Dr. Gregory's migration to Edinburgh is as follows:—

"This (1764) was the year when Dr. John Gregory, my Leyden friend, came to settle at Edinburgh, a widower with three sons and three daughters. He soon came to be perfectly known here, and got into very good business. Dr. Rutherford, Professor of the Practice of Physic, beginning to fail and being afraid of Cullen becoming his successor, whom he held to be an heretic, he readily entered into a compact with Gregory, whom he esteemed orthodox in the medical faith, and resigned his class to him. In a year or two that doctor died, and Cullen and Gregory, agreeable to previous settlement, taught the two classes the theory and practice by turns, changing every session. I got Gregory elected into the Poker, a quaint political club, but though very desirous at first, yet he did not avail himself of it, but deserted after twice attending, afraid, I suppose, of disgusting some of the ladies he paid court to by falling in sometimes there with David Hume whom they did not know for the good soul which he really was. Professor Ferguson told me not long ago that he was present the second time Dr. Gregory attended the Poker, when enlarging on his favourite topic, the superiority of the female sex, he was so laughed at and run down that he never returned."

During his residence at Aberdeen Dr. Gregory was one of the chief founders of a literary society, at which the members, who were for the most part professors at the two Colleges, read essays on literary and philosophical subjects. Although a constant contributor to the proceedings of this society, it was not until about the time of his removal to Edinburgh, that Dr. Gregory ventured upon the publication of any of his writings; and, in fact, it is a curious feature of his literary work that publication does not seem to have been his object in writing, but to have been the result of circumstances.

The death of his wife (in 1763), leaving him with a very young family, seems to have driven him to literary work "for the amusement of his solitary hours," as he himself says,* and probably strengthened his intimacy with his literary associates. From the time, at all events, of his settlement in Edinburgh, Dr. Gregory lived on terms of close intimacy with most of the Scottish *literati* of the time; Drs. Robertson and Blair, David Hume, John Home, Lord Monboddo, and Lord Kaimes appear to have been amongst his especial friends.

---

* See *Father's Legacy*.

The *Father's Legacy to his Daughters*, to which reference has already been made, was written by Dr. Gregory soon after the loss of his wife, and, containing advice to his children which in the event, anticipated by himself, of his own early death he would no longer be able to give them on their entrance into the world, was clearly not intended for publication during the author's lifetime. It was published, after his death, by his son, Dr. James Gregory.

Dr. Gregory's first publication—made in 1764, at the suggestion of Lord Lyttelton—was a work entitled *A Comparative View of the State and Faculties of Man with those of the Animal World*. This work, which was founded on a series of essays read before the Aberdeen Literary Society, attracted considerable attention, and passed through four editions in two years.

In the same year (1764) Dr. Gregory also published a *Life of The Rev. Robert Hall* and *Letters on Literature*.

In 1770 Dr. Gregory published a volume of *Lectures on the Duties and Qualifications of a Physician*. These were the introductory lectures to his annual courses—the only lectures which Dr. Gregory was in the habit of committing fully to writing—and were not written with a view to publication. Many copies, however, were taken by his pupils, and some from the original manuscript, which he freely lent for their perusal. Upon hearing that a copy had been offered for sale to a bookseller, Dr. Gregory forestalled all attempts at piracy by authorising a print from a corrected copy. The profits of the publication he gave to a favourite pupil. The lectures were republished in an enlarged form in 1772.

In 1772 Dr. Gregory also published *Elements of the Practice of Physic*, for the use of students; a work intended solely for his own pupils, and to be used by himself as a text-book to be commented upon in his course of lectures. In an advertisement prefixed to this work he signified his intention of comprehending in it the whole series of diseases of which he treated in his lectures, but this intention he did not live to accomplish.

Dr. Gregory was from his eighteenth year subject to frequent attacks of gout, which he had inherited from his mother, and he seems to have had the apprehension of an early and sudden death from the results of this disease constantly before his mind. In the beginning of the year 1773, when Dr. Gregory had for nearly three years been free from any attack of his complaint, his son James hazarded the observation that after this interval he might "make his account" with a pretty severe attack at that season. Dr. Gregory resented the observation with some degree of warmth, as he felt himself then in his usual state of health; but the prediction was justified by the event, for, on the 10th February 1773, Dr. Gregory was found dead in his bed. His death had been instantaneous and probably in his sleep, for there was not the smallest discomposure of limb or feature.

Lord Woodhouselee says of him:—"He was in person considerably above the middle size. His frame of body was compacted with symmetry, but not with elegance. His limbs were not active; he stooped somewhat in his gait; and his countenance, from a fullness of feature and a heaviness of eye, gave no external indication of superior power of mind or abilities. It was otherwise when engaged in conversation. His features then became animated and his eye most expressive, and he had a warmth of tone and gesture which gave a pleasing interest to everything that he uttered."

The very high tributes which have been paid to the character and abilities of Dr. Gregory in the biographical accounts [*] of him cannot fail to make great impression even on a reader who is prepared to make considerable allowances for the usual pompous character of eighteenth-century expressions on such subjects. The refinement which was so conspicuous in his intellect, we may believe, extended to his moral character, and justified the lament which his friend Beattie introduced into *The Minstrel*, B, ii., 8; v. 61-62.

The most recent account of Dr. Gregory—in Bettany's *Eminent Doctors*—speaks of him thus:—

"His prominent qualities were good sense and benevolence. In conversation he had a warmth of tone and of gesture that were very pleasing, united to a gentleness and simplicity of manner. To his pupils he was a friend, ever easy of access, and ready to assist them to the utmost. ● ● ● As a lecturer he was very successful, simple, and not in any way oratorical in style."

---

[*] More extended quotations would have unduly swelled these Records, and the reader is therefore referred to the Biographies already mentioned.

As a physician and a teacher Dr. Gregory's reputation stands high. He has been termed "one of the most distinguished founders of the Edinburgh School of Medicine" (*Edinburgh Review*, vol. 62, p. 447). But in spite of this distinction, it is as a man of letters that he has left a lasting name.

Although "good sense"* is mentioned as a predominant feature in Dr. Gregory's mind, he was clearly not of the strongest order of scientific intellects, for he confesses that, though he had a hereditary taste for mathematics, he dreaded the study of that science, as "having a tendency to promote scepticism in those matters which do not admit of mathematical evidence." But as an elegant writer and thinker he was entitled to occupy, and obviously did occupy, a very high place.

The *Comparative View* seems to have attracted very considerable notice at the time of its publication, but the work of Dr. John Gregory which was longest remembered was undoubtedly the *Father's Legacy*, the posthumous work already referred to. Sir A. Alison states that this little work was translated into all the languages of Europe. In 1814 Mr. John Gregory (No. XII., *post*, p. 79), writing from Lisbon, and speaking of his introduction to the Austrian Ambassador and his family says: "My name tempted them to ask me whether I was any relation to the author of a book which they considered one of their chief comforts. I soon found that they alluded to the *Legacy*. The delight they expressed in being acquainted with even the grandson of the author was, I must confess, extremely flattering."

The *Legacy* was one of a class of works on morals, which had a large circulation at the end of the last and beginning of this century, but are hardly suited to the tastes of the present time.

It is itself a manual of advice to the author's daughters on the subject of their general moral conduct, and especially with reference to their demeanour and behaviour towards the opposite sex. It was, as already mentioned, written in anticipation of the early death of the author, and of the consequent launch of the young ladies upon the world in a comparatively friendless condition.

---

* Mr. Bettany adopts this phrase from Lord Woodhouselee.

The author's mistrust of friends, of whom he predicts that his daughters will meet with few "disinterested enough to do you good offices when you are incapable of making them any return," was singularly falsified by the event and the kind care afterwards experienced by one at least of his daughters at the hands of Mrs. Montague. It is probably to her, however, that Dr. Gregory alludes as "their mother's friend, to whom they owe so much."

The pamphlet deals with the heads of "Religion," "Conduct and Behaviour," "Amusements," "Friendship, Love, and Marriage," and is full of remarks of great acuteness, pointedly and elegantly expressed. Over-education and deep investigation are treated by Dr. Gregory as objectionable from a religious and social point of view. He deprecates books and conversation tending to shake the faith of his daughters, and also any studies which might make them so over-refined and sensitive that marriage would, except under peculiarly favoured circumstances, be likely to be unhappy. In order to facilitate their choice of husbands he states his intention of leaving them an adequate provision. As to religion, he explains his reason for bringing his daughters up as Episcopalians by reference to the fact that he had "a prejudice of everything liked" by his wife, who "had been educated in the Church of England and had an attachment to it." Dr. Gregory says he looked on the differences between the churches as of no real importance and that a preference of one to the other was a mere matter of taste. It is therefore no matter of surprise that the Kirk did not retain any firm hold upon his descendants.

It is interesting to notice that Dr. John Gregory had a very decided taste for music, as is attested by his regular attendance at the Aberdeen Musical Society, of which he was one of the founders and for many years President.

Dr. John Gregory had the following five children:—

1. James, born 1753, *see below* p. 60.
2. Dorothea Montague, born 11th June 1754, died 6th July 1830, married 19th June 1784 to Rev. Archibald Alison, B.C.L. (born 13th November 1757, died 17th May 1839) a college friend of her brother William, and then rector of Sudbury, Northamptonshire. After her

father's death in 1773, Dorothea Gregory made her home with Dr. John Gregory's friend, Mrs. Montague, who had evinced the greatest affection to her from childhood. Under these good auspices she passed the next ten years of her life in the midst of the most brilliant and intellectual circle in London. A visit to Paris under Mrs. Montague's protection gave her an introduction to all the leading French celebrities of the time immediately preceding the Revolution. Sir Archibald Alison, the second son of Mrs. Alison, also intimates * that his mother resisted the offer of many "brilliant alliances" (one of which would have brought her into affinity with Mrs. Montague herself), and hints that her marriage with Mr. Alison was considered by no means an equal match. Mr. Alison was a protegé of Sir William Pulteney, and through him obtained the livings of Kenley, High Ercal and Rodington, Salop. He was also appointed a Prebendary of Sarum. From 1800 he was for many years Minister of the Cow-Gate Episcopal Chapel, Edinburgh, but without resigning his English preferments. He was the author of a work which acquired great popularity in its day, called *Essays on the Nature and Principles of Taste*. According to Lord Cockburn (*Memorials of his own Time*, p. 305) Mr. Alison was " the most distinguished of the Episcopalian clergy of Edinburgh, and so far as he knew, of Scotland," and he describes him as " a most excellent and agreeable man, richly imbued with literature, and a great associate of Dugald Stewart, Playfair, Dr. Gregory, Jeffrey, and all the eminent among us." They had besides four daughters two sons, viz. : (1) William Pulteney Alison, M.D., F.R.S.E., born 12th November 1790. He held the following Professorships in the University of Edinburgh : Medical Jurisprudence (1820), Institutes of Medicine (1821-1842), Practice of

---

* Autobiography.

Physic (1842-1855). He married his cousin, Margaret Craufurd Gregory,* and died 22nd September 1859, receiving a public funeral from the Corporation of Edinburgh. Of William Pulteney Alison, Sir A. Grant writes †—" Not only was he an eminent Professor, and for a time head of the medical profession in this country (Scotland), but his name deserves to be kept in remembrance as a great philanthropist, and the author of the improved system of the Poor Laws in Scotland." Carlyle calls him ‡ " The brave and humane Dr. Alison, whose noble healing art in his charitable hands becomes once more a truly sacred one." (2) Sir Archibald Alison (created a baronet, 1853), the author of *The History of Europe* and numerous other well-known works. He held for many years the office of Sheriff of Lanarkshire, and earned for himself in that capacity a high reputation both as an able lawyer and a courageous administrator. He died 23rd May 1867. His autobiography, recently published, is several times referred to in the course of these pages.

3. Anna Margaretta, married John Forbes of Blackford, in Aberdeenshire, in 1784, and had issue.
4. William, of whom below, Chapter IX.
5. John, R.N., died 13th March 1783, in the twenty-first year of his age. He had been on service in the West Indies, and was taken prisoner by the Spaniards. Being despatched to England by his captors he was shipwrecked on the Irish coast, and died shortly afterwards at Fahan, in Ireland.
6. Elizabeth, died 1771.

XI. James Gregory, M.D., F.R.C.P., F.R.S.E., eldest son of John Gregory, born 1753, died 1821.

---

* *See below, p. 68.*   † *Story of University of Edinburgh.*
‡ *Past and Present*, Chapter I.

James Gregory was born at Aberdeen in 1753, and seems to have had a very complete education. His father having migrated to Edinburgh, as we have seen, in 1764, James Gregory naturally was sent to the University of Edinburgh, where he went through the arts course. Afterwards he spent some time at Christ Church, Oxford. He acquired a strong taste for classics, and no little classical erudition, so that he was throughout life fond of making apposite Latin quotations, and wrote that language easily and accurately.* He was still a Student of Medicine at Edinburgh when his father's sudden death took place. He then performed the surprising feat of completing his father's unfinished course of lectures for the session 1772-3. In 1774 he took his degree of M.D. at Edinburgh, and then spent two years in medical studies at Leyden and Paris, and in Italy.

In June 1776, being only twenty-three years old, Dr. James Gregory was unanimously elected Professor of the Institutes of Medicine in Edinburgh, in succession to Dr. Cullen who had been transferred to the chair of the Practice of Physic on the death of Dr. John Gregory. The interval of three years between the latter event and Dr. James Gregory's election appears, according to Sir Alexander Grant, to have been wasted, as far as the University was concerned, in an offer of the chair to a certain Dr. Alexander Monro Drummond, who ultimately declined it. Dr. James Gregory's connection as a professor with the University of Edinburgh extended, as we shall see, from his election in 1776 as Professor of the Institutes down to his death, forty-five years later, as Professor of the Practice of Physic. This period corresponds with that which was probably the brightest period in the history of the University of Edinburgh, or at all events of its medical school, and during a great portion of it Dr. James Gregory was decidedly the most conspicuous figure in the medical faculty. Sir Alexander Grant states (*Story of the University of Edinburgh*, II., 269) that "at the end of the last century the faculties of arts and medicine were stronger in their *personnel* than they had ever previously been, and the University of Edinburgh shone out in contrast to the

---

* Bettany, *Eminent Doctors*.

depressed condition of Oxford and Cambridge, and attracted many English students of high rank." The rise in the popularity of the medical school will be seen from the following figures extracted from Sir A. Grant's *Story of the University of Edinburgh*, giving the average of the medical graduations per annum :—

Immediately before 1770	....	12 per annum
1770 to 1784	....	20 ,,
1784 to 1800	....	50 ,,
1800 to 1824	....	100 ,,
1824	....	140 ,,
1827	....	160 ,,

Of these medical graduates a large proportion were not Scotchmen, but were attracted to the University by the reputation of its teaching and the value which the high standard of its examinations gave to its degrees.

In the teaching and examination work of the medical school Dr. James Gregory took a foremost part,* as will be seen from Sir A. Grant's work and the quotations from Sir Robert Christison's Memoirs there given; and at the same time he gradually established himself in practice as a Physician at Edinburgh.

Mr. Bettany says of him:—

"His practice at first was not extensive, until his pupils had themselves become practitioners, and called him in as a consultant. In his later years, after Cullen's death, his practice increased largely, and in the ten years preceding his death he had the leading consulting practice in Scotland."

In 1788, while holding the chair of the Institutes of Medicine, Dr. James Gregory published a text book of his subject called *Conspectus Medicinæ Theoreticæ*, a work which has been described by Dugald Stewart as "a philosophical and elegant work"; and by Sir Robert Christison as "a model of perspicuity, exactness, completeness for the time, and classical elegance." It was for a long time a standard work for examinations at the various examining boards of the kingdom, and was adopted as a text book at some of the German Universities. It has gone through numerous editions, and has been translated into several languages.

---

* From 1777-1797 he gave Clinical Lectures at the Infirmary.

In a few years Dr. James Gregory had so thoroughly established his reputation that, on Dr. Cullen's retirement from active work in 1790, he was appointed his colleague to the chair of the Practice of Physic, with the right of survivorship. After Cullen's death Dr. Gregory remained sole occupant of the chair during the rest of his life. In 1818, however, in consequence of the pressure of his professional practice, he obtained permission to employ his nephew, Dr. W. P. Alison, as an assistant in the delivery of his lectures.

Sir R. Christison says of him: "He was the most captivating lecturer I ever heard. Large, powerful and handsome, he was full of combativeness, and on questions of infirmary management he was involved in deadly life-long feud with many estimable brethren within and beyond the University. His measures for the cure of disease were sharp and incisive. In acute diseases there was no 'medicine expectante' for Gregory. He somehow left us with the impression that we were to be masters over nature in all such diseases. The consequence was that Gregorian physic, free blood-letting, the cold effusion, brisk purging, frequent blisters, the nauseating action of tartar emetic, came to rule medical practice for many years in all quarters throughout the British Islands and the Colonies."

"Gregory's influence," says Sir A. Grant, "has now passed away. Blood-letting, of which he was the apostle, has been superseded; but his name still lives as a household word in connexion with that milder remedy 'Gregory's Mixture.'"

The prominent position long occupied by Dr. Gregory in his profession and his University is so unique, that a recent writer [*] seems justified in speaking of "Gregory's autocracy." The following description of him by the same author deserves quotation in full:—

> "As a teacher Gregory was conspicuous for a sound practicality. He highly approved of a maxim which he often brought forward, 'The best physician is he who can distinguish what he can do from what he cannot do.' Pathology in his day was a very rudimentary science, and hence he distrusted all theories in regard to the essential nature of the disease as premature and visionary. He was at home in the study of diagnostic and prognostic symptoms, and paid considerable attention to the action of

[*] Mr. Bettany.

remedies. He had no tendency to meddlesome medicine, restraining and discountenancing treatment when there was no hope or prospect of success. He believed strongly in the antiphlogistic or lowering treatment of inflammatory diseases, and in the use of preventive measures in warding off the attacks of chronic diseases. Thus he presented the spectacle of an advocate of temperance, of bodily exertion without fatigue, and of mental occupation without anxiety, who by no means followed his own prescriptions.

"As a lecturer he displayed a most ready command of language and an excellent memory, especially for cases he had seen, the details of which he could accurately remember from the name alone of the patient. He gained great influence over the minds of his pupils, not merely by the humour and the abundance of his illustrations, but also by the outspoken exposition of his views and his commanding energy. His frankness showed itself, too, in the candour with which he communicated his opinions to the relatives or friends of his patients. He took a genuine interest in his patients, and convinced them of his sincerity, notwithstanding a certain roughness of manner. Where he felt no personal antagonism he was on very cordial terms with his professional friends, and succeeded in gaining their esteem and regard by his manner towards them in consultation. He was, as we have said before, the admitted autocrat of the profession in Edinburgh in his later years, and it is much to be regretted that his contributions to the science of medicine are so few."

The "combativeness" referred to by Sir R. Christison,* is a characteristic which unfortunately mars the record of Dr. James Gregory's life. It kept him for many years in a continual state of hostility towards the mass of his profession, and in one case led him so far as an assault of one of his academical colleagues; an excess for which he was compelled to pay £100 damages in an action at law.

The infirmary quarrel above mentioned, which took place in 1800, is described by Lord Cockburn, in his *Memorials of His Own Time*, as follows:—

"There appears to have been an absurd arrangement for all Members of Colleges of Physicians and Surgeons to attend the Infirmary at Edinburgh in monthly rotation. Dr. James Gregory, whose learning extended beyond that of his profession, attacked the absurdity in one of his powerful, but wild and personal, quarto pamphlets. The public was entirely on his side, and so, at last, were the managers.

"Gregory, descended from an illustrious line, was a curious and excellent man, a great physician, a great lecturer, a great Latin scholar, and a great

* See p. 63.

talker; vigorous and generous, large of stature, and with a strikingly powerful countenance. The popularity due to these qualities was increased by his professional controversies and the diverting publications by which he used to maintain and enliven them. The controversies were rather too numerous, but they never were for any selfish end, and he was never entirely wrong. Still, a disposition towards personal attack was his besetting sin. Mr. John Bell, the best surgeon that Scotland had then produced, was generally put forward to carry on the Gregorian battles. Perhaps he had the best both of the argument and the clever writing; but the public sided with the best laugher, and so Gregory was generally held to have the victory."

A long list of controversial books and pamphlets by Dr. Gregory is given by Mr. John Bell in his *Letters on Professional Controversy and Manners*, 1810, and apparently is not exhaustive. The bulk of some of these is astounding, and the modern reader cannot but regret the waste of time and money upon productions of this order.

There is, however, abundant testimony from those who knew him that, notwithstanding this defect of "combativeness," he possessed many remarkable and excellent qualities, and won a large share of their attachment and esteem.* Dr. Alison says of him) *Encyclopædia Britannica*, Eighth Edition), "The boldness, originality, and strength of his intellect, and the energy and decision of his character, were strongly marked in his conversation, and he showed both warm attachment to his friends and a generosity almost bordering on profusion. He disdained to conciliate public favour, and often gave unrestrained vent to a strongly irascible temper. He would not give up his point in argument, and would overwhelm his opponents with quotations, jests and satire."

Dr. James Gregory, who was a Fellow of the Royal Society of Edinburgh, was President of the Royal College of Physicians of Edinburgh in 1799. In the latter year he became, like his father, First Physician to the King in Scotland. His commission was renewed by George IV. in 1820.

The extent and value of his professional practice might be seen from passages in his correspondence with his nephew Dr. George Gregory, and the numerous cases for opinion and letters for

---

* Mr. Bottany.

advice, which were until lately preserved amongst the family records. Dr. James Gregory's advice seems to have been sought, not only by practitioners and patients in all parts of the United Kingdom, but by correspondents in Paris, St. Petersburgh, and other places on the Continent. In 1818 his professional income was £2,723, and in the following year £100 more; while in the same years he derived from his professorship by way of fees from pupils £1,364 and £1,200 respectively.

A memorandum is preserved of a fee of £120 having been offered or paid to the doctor for a country visit of only 48 miles distance from Edinburgh.

Dr. Gregory's contribution to the technical literature of his profession was limited to his *Conspectus*, but he devoted part of his leisure to other portions of the field of letters. He used to say that while physic had been the business, metaphysics had been the amusement of his life. His cousin, Dr. Reid, recognised his studies in the latter direction by dedicating to him and Dugald Stewart jointly, his *Essays on the Intellectual Powers*; and Thomas Brown and Dugald Stewart were among his most intimate friends. His publication of an essay on *Motive and Action* [*] led to an acrimonious correspondence with the supporters of the opposite views on the doctrine of liberty and necessity. His philological studies led him to publish in 1787 an essay on the *Theory of the Moods of Verbs*, and, in 1792, he published a collection of literary and philosophical essays. He was also given to the production of epigrams, and translations of poetry from foreign languages, and had a remarkable talent for the composition of epitaphs and inscriptions in Latin. He was the author of the inscriptions on most of the public monuments, &c., erected during his time in Scotland.

Dr. Gregory was an honorary member of numerous literary and scientific societies, such as then existed, including the Speculative Society of Edinburgh (1773), Medical Society of Edinburgh (1773), and Medical Society of Aberdeen; and he was honored by election as a Member of the Institute of France (1817), Royal Medical

---

[*] Jeremy Bentham, on being consulted as to this Essay, objected in very decided terms to "a practical professional man standing forth as an author upon subjects so purely speculative." Letter to G. Wilson, Works X., 215.

Society of Madrid (1787), and Imperial Academy of Sciences of St. Petersburgh. He was also presented with the freedom of the towns or cities of Musselburgh (1779), Limerick (1808), Edinburgh (1815), and Dumfermline (1819).

Dr. Gregory married, in 1781, Mary Ross, who died in April 1784. There was no issue of this marriage.

On 19th October 1796 Dr. Gregory married, secondly, Isabella, daughter of Donald Macleod, of Geanies, Ross-shire, Sheriff of Ross-shire. This lady bore to him a numerous family, and, surviving her husband, died in June 1847, aged 75.

Dr. James Gregory died in April 1821, and received a public funeral from the Corporation of Edinburgh.

Dr. James Gregory had eleven children by his second marriage, viz. :—

1. John, born 10th August 1797. He was admitted advocate in 1820, but never practised. He died unmarried 21st August 1869.
2. Hugh, born 7th June 1799, died at Howden 16th November 1811.
3. James Craufurd, born 5th December 1801. *See* below, p. 68.
4. William, twin with Donald, born 25th December 1803. *See* below, p. 69.
5. Donald, twin with William, was an antiquary of considerable repute, and his work *The Highlands and the Isles of Scotland*, published in 1834, is constantly referred to as a standard authority. He was Secretary to the Antiquarian Society of Scotland, and a Member of the Royal Society of Northern Antiquaries of Copenhagen, and of the Antiquarian Society of Newcastle-upon-Tyne. He was the first Secretary of the Clan Gregor Society.* His publications and work in connection with the history of the clan have been already noticed.* He was originally trained for the profession of the law and became a Writer to the Signet. In 1826, however, he gave up his profession

---
* *See* above, pp. 4-7.

and entered the army as a Second-Lieutenant in the 21st Royal Scots Fusiliers, but he retired from the Service in 1828, finding that his means did not permit of his continuing in it. He then returned to his former vocation, but did not acquire much practice. He died unmarried 21st October 1836.

6. Jane Macleod, eldest daughter, born 15th December 1805, died 27th August 1813 of scarlet fever at Aberdeen, while on a visit there with her parents. She is buried at Aberdeen, and her monument in the Drum's Aisle of St. Nicholas' Church bears an elaborate Latin inscription written by her father.

7. Elizabeth Forbes, born 6th February 1808, died at Edinburgh, 15th March 1811, of scarlet fever.

8. Margaret Craufurd, born 30th November 1809, married 6th September 1832 to her first cousin, Dr. William Pulteney Alison,* son of her father's sister Dorothea. She died 18th December 1849, without issue.

9. Georgina, called Georgina Wilson in certain deeds, but registered as Georgina only, born 15th July 1811, died unmarried 25th June 1877.

10. Duncan Farquharson, born 14th April 1813, died 23rd February 1844. *See* below, p. 71.

11. Isabella, born 19th October 1816, died at Edinburgh January 1818.

XII. James Craufurd Gregory, M.D., F.R.C.P., F.R.S.E., third son of Dr. James Gregory, born 5th December 1801, died 1832.

James Craufurd Gregory, graduated M.D. at Edinburgh in 1824, and afterwards studied in Paris for three years. He became a Fellow of the Royal College of Physicians of Edinburgh in 1828.

The recently published reminiscences of Dr. C. J. Williams, who was a fellow student with Dr. J. C. Gregory, both at Edinburgh and Paris, bear ample testimony to his early promise, and it appears that he was not only a favourite pupil with the anatomist

---

* *See above, p. 60.*

Laennec, but that he was frequently put forward by him to give explanations and make experiments, apparently to the indignation of his fellow students.

On his return to Edinburgh, Dr. Gregory became one of the Physicians to the Royal Infirmary in that city, where he was also a Lecturer; also Ordinary Physician to the Lunatic Asylum, Medical Secretary to the Board of Health, and Superintendent of the Cholera Hospital.

He was also Secretary to the Royal Society of Edinburgh and to the Medico-Chirurgical Society. In 1829 he published an edition of *Cullen's First Lines*, with full notes, and he also contributed several papers to the *Edinburgh Medical Journal*. In 1832 he was a candidate for the Chair of Medical Jurisprudence in the University of Edinburgh, vacated by Dr. (afterwards Sir Robert) Christison, but was defeated by Professor T. S. Traill.

He died unmarried 28th December 1832, of typhus fever, caught in the discharge of his professional duties at the infirmary.

A writer in the *London Medical and Surgical Journal*, January, 1833, says of him: "Dr. Gregory was one of the finest figures we ever saw. His features were regular, and, indeed, truly handsome, and displayed an intelligence and a benevolence rarely observable."

XII. William Gregory, M.D., F.R.C.P., F.R.S.E., fourth son of Dr. James Gregory, and twin with Donald, born 25th December 1803, died April 1858.

William Gregory was educated at the University of Edinburgh, and graduated M.D. in 1828. In 1829 he became a fellow of the Royal College of Physicians of Edinburgh, but he does not seem to have entertained the idea of pursuing medicine as a profession, the bent of his mind being towards chemical science.

An account of Professor William Gregory is given in the late Sir A. Grant's *Story of the University of Edinburgh*, based upon an obituary notice of him published by his brother-in-law and cousin Professor W. P. Alison, in the proceedings of the Royal Society of Edinburgh, 1858:—

"In early youth, while attending the experiments conducted by Dr. Hope, the Professor of Medicine and Chemistry at Edinburgh, William

Gregory was filled with a feeling of emulation, and he is said to have kept steadily before him the idea of becoming his successor. It was not, however, until he had made his name throughout Europe as a chemist, as a favourite pupil and friend of Baron Liebig, and the approved translator of several of his works, and had established his reputation as a teacher of his favourite science in Edinburgh, Glasgow, Dublin,[*] and King's College, Aberdeen, that he at length realised the object of his ambition.

"From the effects of a fever in his youth, Dr. William Gregory, though a large and powerfully-made man, was precluded from much walking, and was condemned to an almost sedentary life. He devoted much of his time to the acquisition of various languages, and to the practice of music (for which he had a refined taste), and to microscopical observations."

From 1839-1844 he was Professor of Chemistry in King's College, Aberdeen, and, on the death of Dr. Charles Hope in 1844 (who had held his chair for 49 years), Dr. William Gregory was appointed his successor as Professor of Chemistry—Medicine, with which the science of Chemistry had theretofore been associated, being removed from that department.

In 1832 Dr. William Gregory was elected a Fellow of the Royal Society of Edinburgh, and at a later period became (like his brother James) one of its Secretaries. He was also Secretary of the Phrenological Society of Edinburgh, a member of the kindred Society in Paris, and a Member of the Societé de Pharmacie de Paris.

According to an account of him in *Chambers' Encyclopædia* (where he is termed "one of the most distinguished chemists of his time") his contributions to the science of chemistry included improved processes for the preparation of hydrochloric acid, muriate of morphia, and oxide of silver, and memoirs on the preparation of sulphuric acid, creatine, &c.

He also contributed several memoirs on Diatomaceæ to the Royal Society of Edinburgh, and published the following larger works:

Translation of Liebig's Animal Chemistry and other works (see *Quarterly Review*, LXX., 98).

Works on Animal Magnetism (see *Ibid*, XCIII., 301).

Outlines of Inorganic Chemistry, of which an American Edition was published by Dr. Saunders in 1851.

---

[*] Where he was Chemical Lecturer at the Park Street Medical School in 1836.

Handbook of Organic Chemistry.
Elementary Treatise on Chemistry.
Liebig's Chemistry in its application to Agriculture and Physiology (published jointly with Dr. Lyon Playfair).
Letters to a Candid Enquirer on Animal Magnetism.

As will be seen from the foregoing list of his works Dr. William Gregory devoted much of his attention to Mesmerism and Animal Magnetism, while Spiritualism was the subject of a considerable, if not excessive, amount of devotion on his part.

Dr. William Gregory died at Edinburgh on 24th April 1858, and (like his father) was honoured by the Corporation with a public funeral. He was succeeded in his chair by his friend Dr. (now Sir) Lyon Playfair, who had unsuccessfully competed against him on his election in 1844.

In June 1839 Dr. William Gregory married Lisette Scott,* daughter of John Scott, Esq., H.E.I.C.S., by whom he had an only son, viz. :—

> James Liebig Gregory, born May 1840, and named after his father's friend and instructor Baron Liebig. He died 5th May 1863, having married (17th September 1861) Elizabeth Mary Somerville Fairfax,† only daughter of Sir Henry Fairfax, Baronet. The only child of this marriage was Henry Makdougall John Fairfax Gregory, born 29th November 1862, died 21st June 1881.

XII. Duncan Farquharson Gregory, the tenth child of Dr. James Gregory, born 1813, died 1844.

Duncan Farquharson Gregory, who was born in Edinburgh 14th April 1813, gave at an early age manifest proofs of considerable natural aptitude for the acquisition of mechanical knowledge. In October 1825 he began attendance at the Edinburgh High School, but when, in 1827, his mother and sisters went to reside temporarily in Switzerland, he was removed from Edinburgh,

---

* Commonly known as Mrs. Makdougall Gregory. Her father's brother was Colonel Scott of Gala. She died 24th May 1883.

† This lady married (September 1884) Lieutenant-Colonel William Marshall Cochrane.

and his education was continued at an academy in Geneva. On the return of the family to Edinburgh, Duncan Farquharson Gregory attended classes at the University of Edinburgh for a short while, and then in 1833 entered at Trinity College, Cambridge. He graduated in the Mathematical Tripos of 1837 as Fifth Wrangler. In 1840 he became a Fellow of Trinity College, Cambridge, and after taking his degree as M.A. in 1841 filled the office of Moderator in the Mathematical Tripos of that year, and of Examiner in the year following.

An anonymous writer, who has discussed the hereditary qualities of the family, speaks of the mathematical talent, which had been practically latent since the time of James Gregorie the astronomer, as "blazing forth" again in Duncan Farquharson Gregory, and it is certainly true that the latter had mathematical gifts of the highest order, which his early death (in 1844) prevented from being fully developed; but even in the brief span of his life he accomplished much work in the sphere of pure mathematics, the sterling value of which is demonstrated by the number and reputation of his mathematical writings.

It appears to have been considered that his taste for general scientific subjects prevented him from devoting himself to the regular curriculum with the exclusive attention necessary to secure the highest places of the Tripos. Probably also his health would not have permitted the strain of more severe uninterrupted study, and it must also be remembered that his competitors were men of highest mathematical rank—Professor Sylvester being Second Wrangler, and Mr. Green (then a man of comparatively mature age) Fourth Wrangler in the same year.

Mr. Gregory's scientific tastes showed themselves in his being one of the founders of, and lecturers before, the Cambridge Chemical Society, and by his acting, while an undergraduate, as assistant to the Professor of Chemistry, but by the time he had taken his degree his mind had been irrevocably attracted to pure mathematics. In this branch of study he developed to a considerable extent the theory of the "combination of symbols," the laws of which had previously been only grasped in a tentative manner by the minds of mathematicians.

His work on this subject appeared first in the shape of contributions to the *Cambridge Mathematical Journal*, of which he was one of the founders and, in fact, the first editor, continuing to hold that office until shortly before his death. "The intrinsic value of his articles, by which in a great degree a spirit of originality was awakened in the University of Cambridge at an era of peculiar stagnation in mathematical invention," induced his friend Mr. William Walton, of Trinity Hall, Cambridge, to republish them in a collected form in 1865.

In 1841 Mr. Gregory published his *Collection of Examples of the Processes of the Differential and Integral Calculus*, a most important contribution to the development of the great instruments employed in mathematical work, and he left unfinished a treatise on *Solid Geometry*, which was published after his death by Mr. Walton. The work on the *Differential and Integral Calculus* remains still a standard text book at Cambridge, while the *Solid Geometry* was in 1870 the best elementary introduction to the subject which had been produced.

Mr. Gregory's reputation rests upon these works, as he did not live to hold any high University position. He was a candidate for the Mathematical Chair at Edinburgh in 1838, while still only a B.A. scholar of Trinity, but was defeated by Professor Kelland, and in 1841 he was offered, but declined, the Mathematical Professorship at Toronto. An estimate of his character and abilities will be found prefixed to the edition of his mathematical writings already referred to, written by his college friend, Mr. R. L. Ellis.

An account of him is also inserted in the *Encyclopædia Britannica*.

Mr. Duncan Farquharson Gregory died unmarried at Canaan Lodge, Edinburgh, on the 23rd of February 1844.

CHAPTER IX.

THE ABERDEEN AND EDINBURGH BRANCH (*continued*).

Having now traced out the descendants of Dr. James Gregory (No. XI.), down to their actual extinction, we return to the next in order and only remaining branch of the family, viz., that sprung from Dr. John Gregory's second son, William.

XI. The Reverend William Gregory, born 1761, died 1803.

William Gregory was educated first at Glasgow University, and afterwards at Balliol College, Oxford (matriculated 10th December 1776, B.A. 1780, M.A. 1783). Among his friends at Balliol were the Reverend Archibald Alison, who afterwards married his sister Dorothea Gregory as mentioned above, the eminent physician Dr. Matthew Baillie, and Dr. Lindsay, afterwards Bishop of Kildare. Mr. Gregory was ordained in 1783, and in 1786 was presented by the Archbishop of Canterbury to the United Rectories of St. Andrew and St. Mary Breadman in Canterbury. In 1788 the same patron appointed him Master of Eastbridge Hospital, in right of which he presented himself to the Vicarage of Blean, Kent. He was afterwards appointed one of the "Six Preachers" in Canterbury Cathedral. On 13th May 1788 he was married at Canterbury Cathedral to Catharine, second daughter of George Sayer,* of Pett Place, Charing, Kent. Mrs. Gregory was born 9th June, and baptized 7th July 1750 at Charing. She died 14th January 1816, and was buried with her husband.

An accident in early youth, while playing cricket, rendered Mr. Gregory lame for life, and his constitution is spoken of as "evincing debility." He died "at his house in the Archbishop's palace" at Canterbury on 31st January 1803, and is buried in the South Cloister of the Cathedral, a tablet bearing his name being placed on the wall of the Cloister. An obituary notice of him appeared in

---

* This George Sayer, who died 17th September 1778, was the grandson of George Sayer, who acquired the estate of Pett by marriage (1st October 1685) with his cousin Frances Honywood, heiress of Sir Philip Honywood of that place.

the *Gentleman's Magazine*, LXXIII., 196, in which his character is drawn in the most eulogistic terms.

The Reverend William Gregory had five children, viz.:—

1. James, born in the Precincts at Canterbury, 22nd March 1787, and admitted as a King's Scholar in the King's School at Canterbury 1797. From the King's School he went, after his father's death, to Edinburgh, where he resided in the house of his uncle Dr. James Gregory, and continued his education at the High School. In 1805 the Bishop of Kildare (Dr. Lindsay), his father's college friend, undertook the cost of his education at Trinity College, Dublin, whither James Gregory proceeded, living during his University career in the house of his patron. He then obtained a scholarship in 1809, and took the usual degrees of B.A. and M.A. in due course. Being ordained about the same time, he became tutor in the family of the Bishop of Kildare and Curate of St. Mary's, Dublin, and then Rector of Lea Portarlington. He next officiated for five years as Curate of St. John's, Edinburgh, and then returning to Dublin became Rector of St. Bridget's in that city. He held the Prebend of Harristown in the Cathedral of Dublin 1823-38, and in 1834 became Dean of Kildare. James Gregory was unfortunately afflicted with deafness, from which he suffered from the 25th year of his age. He married, first, Jane Begbie, who died in 1848, and, secondly, Octavia Letitia, youngest daughter of Sir Thomas Fetherston, Bart., M.P., who survived him. Dean Gregory, who had no issue, died 5th March 1859, and his widow 2nd October 1868.

2. George, of whom below.

3. Catherine, born at Canterbury, December 1791, died unmarried 27th June 1846.

4. William, born in the Precincts, 6th April 1794. He was admitted a King's Scholar in the King's School in 1801, and on the 20th July 1813 received a commission

in the Royal Engineers.* He served for several years in Canada, where he was severely frost-bitten and lost part of his toes from the effects. From 1826-31 he served in Barbadoes. On his voyage to the West Indies he was shipwrecked, and displayed great courage and resource on the occasion.† He became a captain 6th October 1831, and three years later went to Ceylon, where he remained nine years. In 1845, after his return to England, he retired from the Army in consequence of ill-health induced by his long foreign service. From this time until his death, on 17th November 1853, he remained in an almost helpless condition. Captain Gregory never married.

5. John, of whom below.

XII. George Gregory, M.D., F.R.C.P., second son of the Rev. William Gregory, born 1790, died 1853.

George Gregory was born at Canterbury 16th August 1790, and educated at the King's School (1796-1803), and afterwards at the Edinburgh University. He made an early choice of medicine as his profession, and in 1809, through the kindness of his father's friend Dr. Baillie, who bore the cost of his residence in London for the purpose, he was enabled to pursue his studies at St. George's Hospital, and other medical schools of the Metropolis. In 1811 he returned to Edinburgh, and in company with Mr. (afterwards Sir Henry) Holland and his own cousin, W. P. Alison, prepared for and received his degree of M.D. (12th September 1811).

On 3rd July 1812 he obtained by examination his diploma as Member of the Royal College of Surgeons of England, and shortly

---

* *See* above, p. 4.

† Captain Gregory's immense height (6 ft. 7 in.) gave rise to a joke, in reference to the shipwreck, amongst his brother officers, according to whom Captain Gregory reported to the War Office that, after despatching his fellow-sufferers in boats, &c., he himself *waded* on shore in safety! The characteristic height of this branch of the family may here be noted. Dr. James Gregory and his sons were all over 6 ft., and some considerably above that height. Dean Gregory was 6 ft. 1 in., Dr. George Gregory 6 ft. 4 in., and their brother John 6 ft. 2 in. In the descendants of the latter two brothers the standard of height has been well maintained, and one of Dr. George Gregory's grandsons is 6 ft. 7 in. and another 6 ft. 4 in.

afterwards entered the Army Medical Service as "Hospital Assistant to the Forces." Efforts were made to procure for Dr. Gregory immediate appointment to a higher rank in the service, on the score of his academical and other qualifications, but the official rules could not be broken through. In 1813 Dr. Gregory was sent to the Mediterranean and served the following three years with different corps in Sicily and Italy. In April 1814 he took part in the expedition against Genoa under Lord William Bentinck, and was present at the attack on the forts which led to the capitulation of the town and its evacuation by the French.

On the termination of the hostilities and his return to England in 1816 he quitted the army, and after passing the L.R.C.P. examination at the Royal College of Physicians of England, commenced practice as a physician in London. He became a Fellow of the Royal College of Physicians of England 30th September 1839. From February 1817 to May 1829 he was Physician to St. George's and St. James' Dispensary, subsequently becoming Consulting Physician to that institution, of which he was for many years Treasurer (1841-1853).

In 1822, Dr. Gregory became Physician to the Small-pox and Vaccination Hospital at Highgate, and from that date devoted himself very largely to the study and cure of febrile and eruptive disorders, on which he became a leading authority.

His work as a teacher commenced with lectures on the practice of physic, delivered at the Medical School, in Little Windmill Street, and in 1840 he became a lecturer at St. Thomas' Hospital.[*] At St. Thomas' he three times delivered the customary inaugural lecture on the opening of the annual medical course.

Dr. Gregory was an active member of the Westminster Medical Society from its foundation in 1809, and of the Royal Medical and Chirurgical Society of London from 1834, and served as Secretary and on the Council of both these societies.

He displayed a great deal of the literary power of his uncle, Dr. James Gregory, but also like him he had a strong element of combativeness in his character, and became involved in

---

[*] As a lecturer, he "for many years commanded a large and remunerative class."—*Roll of College of Physicians.*

controversies, especially on subjects of professional reform. His contributions to periodical literature were exceedingly numerous. He was the author of frequent articles in the *London Medical Gazette, Medical Times, Lancet,* &c., &c., and was a contributor to the *Cyclopædia of Practical Medicine* and to the *Library of Medicine.*

In 1819 he published a volume of *Lectures on Dropsy,* and in 1820 he brought out a work entitled *Elements of the Theory and Practice of Medicine,* which ran through six editions in England and two in America. This book was officially adopted and recommended by the medical authorities of the army.

In 1843, Dr. Gregory published *Lectures on the Eruptive Fevers,* an edition of which, with additions, was published in New York by Dr. Bulkeley in 1851.

In 1841, Dr. Gregory was a candidate for the Chair of Medicine at Glasgow, but was defeated by Dr. Thomson.

Like some other members of the family, Dr. George Gregory had a strong taste for music, and attained considerable skill and ease in composition as well as execution.

Towards middle-age, Dr. Gregory became affected with heart-disease, and after a slight paralytic seizure in 1852, was attacked by *angina pectoris.* He died 25th January 1853.

Dr. Gregory married Frances, daughter of John Le Grice, Esq., of Bury St. Edmunds, and by her (who died 1st May 1839, aged 44), had the following issue :—

1. Frederick William ; born 11th January 1831. He was educated at the King's School, Canterbury, and entered the Army in 1848, obtaining a commission as Ensign in the 44th Regiment. His later commissions were dated as follows : Lieutenant, 24th March 1853 ; Captain, 19th June 1855 ; Brevet-Major, 15th February 1861 ; Regimental-Major, 3rd September 1870 ; Brevet Lieutenant-Colonel, 29th December 1871. According to Hart's *Army List* his services were as follows:— " Served in the Eastern (Crimean) Campaign of 1854-6 with 44th Regiment, including battles of Alma and Inkerman, siege and fall of Sebastopol, attack and occupation of the Cemetery on 18th June (medal with

three clasps, 5th class of Medjidie, and Turkish medal). Served also in the campaign in the North of China, 1860-1, including the action of Sinho, storm and capture of the Taku Forts (medal, with clasps, and Brevet of Major)." Lieutenant-Colonel Gregory retired from the 44th on half-pay in 1871, and in 1878 he sold out of the army. He married, 21st December 1869, Elizabeth Ann, daughter of William Merry, Esq., and had issue three daughters:—(1) Eva Janie, born 27th June 1871, died 12th September 1871; (2) Dorothy Janet; (3) Elsie Millicent. Lieutenant - Colonel Gregory died at Southwold, on 7th September 1884.

2. John Arthur, R.N., born 18th June 1833; educated at King's College, London; entered the Navy 1846 and served on the African Coast. In the winter of 1846-7 he navigated a prize schooner from Cape Lopez to St. Helena—a voyage which, owing to contrary winds and other difficulties, lasted 68 days — without a chronometer, reaching his destination short of provisions. He died of fever, contracted in Africa, at Malta, 22nd December 1849.

3. Harriet Margaret, married to Edward Brown Fitton, and has issue.

4. Isabella Catherine, married to Robert Arthur Whitting, and has issue.

5. Infant son, died 1839, soon after his birth.

XII. John Gregory, fourth son of The Reverend William Gregory, born 1795, died 1853.

John Gregory was born in the Precincts at Canterbury on the 26th October 1795, and in 1804 he was admitted as a King's Scholar in the King's School at Canterbury, where he remained until 1811. In October of the latter year his uncle, Dr. James Gregory, who had already provided in a great degree for the education of his two elder nephews, James and George, also took the youngest, John, into his house and sent him to the classes at the High School of Edinburgh, where his aptitude for mathematics was especially noticed by his instructor, Professor Leslie, as well as by Dr. Gregory himself.

The future in life of John Gregory seemed a difficult problem to solve. He had a decided aversion to the army, in regard to which his mother appears to have had some interest, and his natural inclinations were towards the Church or Medicine. Want of interest and money seemed to bar the way in the former, while his elder brother George having chosen the latter, the entry of the younger brother into the same line was considered objectionable.

In these circumstances John Gregory was glad to accept, in May 1813, a temporary place in the pay department of the army in Portugal, which had been obtained for him through the influence of his mother's early friend, the (seventh) Earl of Bridgwater.

In 1814 Mr. John Gregory, who till then was employed at Lisbon, was recalled to London and was there engaged for a year and a half in assisting to wind up the financial accounts of the Peninsular War.

The general reduction of the army departments which followed threw Mr. John Gregory out of employment for a few months, but, in December 1815, through the same interest as before, he obtained an appointment in the Paymaster-General's Department at Malta. After eighteen months in this appointment he was transferred to Gibraltar, by way of promotion, as Deputy-Paymaster-General, where he remained five years in charge of the Paymaster-General's Department. During a great part of this latter period he served as Commissioner for settling disputed titles to landed property, and fixing quit-rents.

In December 1821 Mr. John Gregory returned home and, on the further reduction of the military establishments, was, as one of the juniors, discharged from the department upon a pension.

In the following July (1822), again through the influence of Lord Bridgwater, he obtained the appointment of Secretary to a Commission which was sent out to enquire into the financial condition of the Eastern Colonies.

For the next nine years Mr. Gregory was employed on this Commission, spending four years (1823-7) at the Cape of Good Hope, two years (1827-9) at Mauritius, and two years (1829-31) in Ceylon.

Mr. Gregory returned from Ceylon in 1831 and, after winding up the affairs of the Commission in London, obtained from Lord Ripon (then Lord Goderich) the appointment of Colonial Treasurer in Van Diemen's Land, with a seat in the Executive and Legislative Councils (12th March 1833).

This colony, which was then a penal settlement, was under the government of Colonel (afterwards Sir George) Arthur, on whose retirement, in 1837, Sir John Franklin (afterwards celebrated for his memorable Arctic voyage) succeeded as Lieutenant-Governor.

Shortly after his arrival (viz., 6th May 1834) Mr. Gregory married Harriet Elizabeth Jean,* a lady of Jersey extraction and daughter of Captain Philip Jean, 21st Royal Scots Fusiliers, whose regiment was then quartered in the colony.

The relations between Mr. Gregory and Sir John Franklin were at first most harmonious, and Mr. Gregory was in fact his confidential adviser; but this state of things was not destined to exist long. It is unnecessary, however, in this place, to go into the various causes and influences which combined to destroy the position acquired by Mr. Gregory in the confidence of his superior, and the intrigues which ultimately broke up the *personnel* of the Colonial Government. The climax was reached in 1839 in relation to what was locally known as the "Feigned Issue" Bill. In the previous year (1838) the Government had introduced a measure prohibiting distillation within the colony, and of this (as it was, to a certain extent, a revenue measure) Mr. Gregory had charge. In accordance with the directions of the Government, Mr. Gregory publicly announced that in the following year a measure would be introduced providing for compensation to be paid to the local distillers whose trade was destroyed; and on the faith of this promise the prohibitory Bill was passed by the local legislature. However, when the Session of 1839 came, it was found that the compensation measure† introduced by the Government ostensibly to fulfil Mr. Gregory's

---

* She died 10th April 1867, aged 56.

† The Bill was framed during the absence of Mr. Gregory from the Executive Council, from which his name had, by a copyist's error, been omitted on the issue from the Colonial Office of the warrant reconstituting the Council on the demise of the Crown. On 5th February 1840 a despatch was received explaining the mistake, and restoring Mr. Gregory, but the Governor, on his own responsibility, suspended him until the decision of the main dispute had been received.

pledge proposed that before any compensation should be paid to any distiller an issue should be sent to the local Court of Justice to try whether or not the distillery had been conducted contrary to law. This portion of the Bill was a limitation of the right of compensation, which had never been suggested before, and was accordingly considered, both by Mr. Gregory and the colonial public, as a breach of the pledge previously given.

To the Government measure in this form Mr. Gregory offered (as he considered himself in honour and duty bound to do) a strenuous opposition, and it was thrown out in the Legislative Council by a majority of two votes. The propriety of Mr. Gregory's conduct in thus opposing the Government of which he was a member, was at once (September 1839) referred to the Colonial Office in London.

The Secretary of State in his despatch in answer (received August 1840) avoided an actual judgment on Mr. Gregory, but intimated that Sir John Franklin, by virtue of his authority as Governor, had full power to remove him from his office of Treasurer if he considered such a step necessary for carrying on the Government. Of this power Sir John Franklin promptly availed himself.

The result of Mr. Gregory's removal from office was of course his immediate departure from the colony (20th October 1840)—not, however, before he had received a testimony of the deep regret at his departure felt by his fellow-citizens in an address, signed by 240 residents, recording his public services and the appreciation felt by the colony of his character and abilities.

It may be mentioned that Mr. Gregory was not the first important official who had been removed from office in the colony, and that the power of removal proved a fatal gift to Sir John Franklin. It was next used by him against his Colonial Secretary; and the enquiries which were necessitated by the dismissals of the two senior officials in the colony resulted in such dissatisfaction on the part of the home authorities with Sir John Franklin's administration that he was forthwith recalled (Despatch, 10th February 1843).

As regards the Bill itself, the final cause of the evils which had fallen upon Mr. Gregory, it was referred to, and wholly disapproved by, the Home Government. The final instructions which were sent out to Sir John Franklin upon the matter were based upon the very principle contended for by Mr. Gregory, viz., that the distillers were entitled to receive the compensation already promised them, without the ordeal of any trial whatever.

This complete approval and justification of the principles and action adopted by Mr. Gregory was, however, very slight satisfaction to him for the loss of his office, and he was destined to wait many years in inactivity before being again employed in the service of the Crown.

Mr. Gregory had not sufficient political interest with the party for the time being in power to obtain an early offer of an appointment which he considered worthy of his acceptance, although some minor appointments were from time to time offered to him. At last his continued applications resulted (18th November 1848) in his appointment by Lord Grey as Governor of the Bahama Islands, whither on 2nd February 1849 he proceeded.

On assuming his government Mr. Gregory's first task was to make a general tour of inspection of the islands under his charge, for the purpose of acquiring a knowledge of the grievances of the outlying communities, by way of preparation for his first meeting with the Colonial Legislature in February 1850.

The public difficulties with which Mr. Gregory in this, and the subsequent sessions of his miniature Parliament had to deal, were chiefly financial. The colony was then in a very elementary stage of development, with very slight industries, and an export-trade chiefly consisting of pineapples, oranges, and limes, and it taxed all the ingenuity of its Governor to make its tiny revenue of about £22,000, which depended greatly on the wreckage cast up on the shores of the islands, cover its expenditure. However, Mr. Gregory did not hesitate to ask for the abolition of the export fruit duty, and for the reduction of the tonnage duties on shipping,— two points on which he found the existing laws press hardly upon the "out-islands;" and he was equally bold in demanding an increase of the education grant. The special interest of Mr. Gregory in education is shown by the constant recurrence in his speeches to this subject, and by the expressions of his regret at the inadequate response made to his propositions for increased liberality in the education grants. He had, indeed, made a point of personally inspecting the schools and examining the children, and he never lost an opportunity of enforcing by his public utterances the duty of giving prominence to the religious side of educational work.

Amongst other matters specially noticed by Mr. Gregory as requiring Legislative attention were the Parliamentary representation of the "out-islands," and the appointment of Stipendiary Magistrates in the same districts; improved provision for sick and lunatic paupers, and the readjustment of the burden of road repairs.

The year 1850 was signalised by a terrible tornado, which on the 30th March swept over the islands and destroyed life and property to a large extent. The Governor had a vast amount of destitution and misery to cope with, and for this purpose he obtained pecuniary help, not only from the Local Legislature, but from the Home Government and the other West India Islands.

The salubrity of the climate of the islands suggested to the Governor the idea of attracting to them invalids from the United States, and the great advantage which the inhabitants would derive from their visitors. Although Mr. Gregory's plans for improving the communication between Nassau and the mainland temporarily failed, his ideas were afterwards fully realised, and numbers of invalids have, in recent years, resorted to Nassau from more northern latitudes.

A work of great local importance, which Mr. Gregory had perceived to be necessary, was also accomplished in 1850 (viz.): the collection in a single volume of the *Statute Law of the Bahamas*.

The Bahamas Legislature met again on 11th February 1851, and, besides the usual financial matters, had to consider the sanitary provisions necessary as a protection against the cholera then raging in other parts of the West Indies.

The financial changes introduced in 1850 had hardly had time to produce their proper effect, and the extreme necessity of economy induced the Legislature, much to Mr. Gregory's dissatisfaction, to refuse a further increase of the education grants for which he asked.

The propositions made by the Governor for the Session of 1852 which, notwithstanding an improvement in the fruit trade, met (4th February) again under pressure of financial difficulties, included the building of a church and maintenance of a clergyman at Inagua—a proposition which gave rise to severe opposition—and a scheme for the control of the salt ponds by means of an elective body on the principles of local self-government.

During this Session two other interesting and important subjects were brought forward by the Governor. The first was another step in his schemes for developing the colony (viz.): measures to convert Nassau, by improving its harbour, into a rendezvous or station for the Royal Navy. The second, made on the suggestion of the Home Government, was the encouragement, by a mitigation of the alien laws, of the immigration of American negroes. This latter proposal found little favour, and was only accepted in a very modified form.

In this Session some technical improvements were made in the laws relating to the administration of justice, and at the prorogation (27th March) the Governor was able to make the satisfactory announcement that the revenue, which in 1850 was £22,027, had risen in 1851 to £24,270, and in 1852 to £26,104.

Immediately after this Session the first period of Mr. Gregory's service in the Bahamas was brought to a close, when he returned to England on six months' leave of absence (April 1851).

The foregoing sketch of the Parliamentary history of the colony will indicate in some degree the way in which Mr. Gregory set himself to discharge his duties and the views which regulated his conduct. That his earnest desire to promote the welfare of the community was appreciated by the colonial public is shown by the collection of addresses presented to him on leaving the colony, and the expressions of respect and admiration used in them regarding his work.

Mr. Gregory returned to Nassau in November 1851, and found many difficulties awaiting him, owing to the epidemic of cholera then raging in the islands, to which 6.4 per cent. of the population fell victims. He met the complaints of official inaction by at once on his arrival instituting a strict house-to-house visitation, and by adopting every possible precaution during the continuance of the epidemic, at a cost of a considerable addition (£4,000) to the public expenditure.

On the 23rd February 1853 Mr. Gregory again met his "Parliament," and in spite of the unfavourable circumstances of the time, urged upon them the matters which he had so much at heart, viz., education and the development of the colony.

But Mr. Gregory's career was destined to be cut short most abruptly. An attack of West Indian fever seized him on the 26th July 1853 and death supervened on the 29th. His funeral, which was public, took place with full honours on the 30th.

It is understood that Mr. Gregory, who on his visit to England in 1852 had declined knighthood, was designated for the Government of Madras, the offer of that appointment being on its way to Nassau at the time of his death.

Mr. Gregory had five children:—

1. Henrietta Catherine.
2. Louisa Arthur, married to the Rev. William Nash, and has issue.
3. John Philip, born in Van Diemen's Land 8th March 1839. He was educated at Rugby (August 1853-1858). Thence he went to University College, Oxford, where he graduated B.A., taking 3rd Class honours in Law and History, 1861, M.A. 1864. He was called to the Bar at Lincoln's Inn 1866, and died 16th November 1869 unmarried.
4. William Villeneuve, Major R.A.
5. Philip Spencer, a Barrister of Lincoln's Inn, married 9th August 1876, to Edith Annie, third daughter of the late Rev. Edward James, Rector of Hindringham, Norfolk, and has one son, John Duncan.

SUPPLEMENTARY CHAPTER.

THE ARMORIAL BEARINGS.

> "Latet arbore opaca
> Aureus et foliis et lento vimine ramus,
> Junoni infernæ dictus sacer ; hunc tegit omnis
> Lucus, et obscuris claudunt convallibus umbræ.
> Sed non ante datur telluris operta subire,
> Auricomos quam qui decerpserit arbore fetus.
> Hoc sibi pulchra suum ferri Proserpina munus
> Instituit. Primo avolso *non deficit alter*
> Aureus, et simili frondescit virga metallo."
> VERGIL, ÆNEID, VI. 136-144.

THE history of the armorial bearings worn by the family of Gregory is involved in obscurity.

It is generally accepted that a fir-tree or pine was the distinctive device of the numerous clans or families once known collectively as "Clan Alpin"; but at some time, not capable of being satisfactorily fixed, the Clan Gregor substituted an oak for the pine. In Douglas' *Baronage of Scotland*, an account is given of the origin of this substitution on the authority of a Latin history of Clan Alpin, recovered from the Scots College at Paris. The hero of the story* is Sir Malcolm Macgregor, who died in 1164, and is mentioned above (p. 7). His descendant, in the eleventh generation, is the first who bore the surname of Gregorie. Douglas' account is as follows :—

> "Sir Malcolm was a man of incredible strength of body. Being of the King's retinue at a certain hunting party in a forest, his Majesty,† having attacked a wild boar or some other animal of prey, was like to be worsted and in great danger of his life, when Sir Malcolm coming up demanded his Majesty's permission to encounter it, and the King having hastily answered, ' In ' (or ' E'en ') ' do, bait spair nocht,' Sir Malcolm is said to have torn up a young oak by the roots, and, throwing himself between his Majesty and the fierce assailant, with the oak in one hand kept the animal at bay till, with the other, he got an opportunity of running it through the heart. In honour whereof his Majesty was pleased to raise him to the peerage by the title of Lord Macgregor, to him " et heredibus masculis," and, in order to

---

* This is the story referred to *supra*, p. 5.   † David I.

perpetuate the remembrance of the brave action, gave him an oak-tree eradicate in place of the fir-tree which the family had formerly carried.

"We have his arms blazoned by an excellent ancient herald in these words:—

"'LORD MACGREGOR OF OLD.—Argent, a sword in bend, azure, and an oak tree eradicate in bend sinister proper; in chief a crown, gules.

"'Crest: A lyon's head, crowned with an antique crown with points.

"'Motto: "In do, bait spair nocht."

"'Supporters: On the dexter an unicorn argent, crowned, horned, or, and on the sinister a deer proper, tyned, azure.'"

The objection to the acceptance of this tradition is, that it places the grant of the arms at a date anterior to that at which, according to more certain authorities, armorial bearings were first worn in Scotland. However, the different families who now bear the name of Macgregor, wear arms very similar to those above described.†

The Gregories, on the other hand, and some other families descended from the Clan Gregor, have adhered to the fir.

On 10th September 1766 a grant of arms was obtained by Dr. John Gregory (above, No. X.) from the Lyon office, as follows‡ :—

"Argent, a fir-tree growing out of a mount in base, vert; surmounted of a sword in bend supporting an imperial crown in the dexter canton, proper; and in chief and base a lyon's head, erazed, azure, armed and langued gules.

"Above the shield a helmet befitting his degree, with a mantling, gules, doubling argent; and on a wreath of his colours§ is set for crest a sphere, and in an escrol above, the motto, 'Altius.'"

The *Arms* as thus described have been accepted and worn by Dr. John Gregory's descendants, and are shown in the first and

---

* The motto of Clan Alpin, according to Douglas, was "Srioghail M'dhream"—"My Tribe is Royal."

† *Berry's Heraldry* gives the Macgregor arms with a fir-tree and a totally different crest. *Guillim*, edition 1724, gives the fir-tree. The grants to the present families of Macgregors (Baronets) are modern. The fir-tree, with sword in bend supporting a crown, is also given by *Papworth* (*Ordinary of British Armorials*), as contained in the arms of Grierson (Scotland), and Grierson (Ireland); and two of the forms of Macgregor arms given by him have the fir-tree.

‡ The form is one of registration, or "matriculation," rather than of a new grant.

§ The colours are white and green, and the wreath in the drawing on the grant is so coloured.

third quarters of the shield on the title-page of these Records.* But immediately on Dr. John Gregory's death a return was made to what is understood to have been the earlier *Crest and Motto*,† viz.: the stump of a tree with a single branch, and the motto, "Nec deficit alter." In adopting the sphere as a crest, and the motto "Altius," it seems that Dr. Gregory, by a "conceit," referred to his own removal from Aberdeen to the "higher sphere" of Edinburgh, as well as to his grandfather's eminence as an astronomer.

The only other grant of arms made in favour of the family is one dated in 1788 by the Lyon office to David Gregorie of Dunkirk (No. X., p. 43, *ante*), in which the *Arms* are the same as in Dr. John Gregory's grant, with the exception that the lyons' heads are omitted. But the grant gives "for crest, the trunk of an old fir-tree fallen, from which issues a vigorous shoot proper, and the motto, 'Non deficit alter.'"

The Dunkirk branch did not, however, strictly adhere to the bearings sanctioned by this grant. The seal on a letter written in 1822 by Mr. John Gregorie of Dunkirk (generation XI., p. 44, *ante*) has the arms in accordance with the grant, but the crest is a lion's head, as in the traditional Macgregor grant, and the motto is the old Clan-Alpin boast, "Srioghal mo' dhram."

The old seals in the possession of Colonel C. F. Gregorie, representing the St. Andrew's Branch (Chapter VI.), give for arms a fir-tree growing out of a mount, with sword in bend, *passing behind the tree*, and supporting a crown, but no "lyons' heads" or other "charges." The crest appears to be the same as that in the Dunkirk grants, viz.: a fir-tree fallen, with a vigorous shoot, and the motto is "Non deficit alter."

The letter of 8th August 1741 ascribed to Professor James Gregorie (*supra*, p. 39) bears a seal with the arms identically corresponding with Dr. John Gregory's grant, except that the

---

* The shield itself contains the full bearings of Dr. John Gregory's family. Dr. Gregory's wife became one of the co-heiresses of the thirteenth Lord Forbes (see page 51), and the Forbes' arms—azure, three bears' heads argent, muzzled gules—are therefore quartered.

† Berry's *Heraldry*, in a supplement, gives for Gregory (Scotland), M.D., arms as in the grant and crest the trunk of an oak-tree shooting out branches vert.

sword is inverted, passing *downwards* across the tree instead of upwards, and supporting the crown on its hilt. The crest given is a stump shooting out branches, similar to that in the woodcut on the title-page, and the motto, "Nec deficit alter." *

It thus appears that in the devices of four branches of the family the same features appear, viz. :—

1. *Arms:* a fir-tree, surmounted by a sword in bend supporting a crown ;
2. *Crest:* a tree shooting out a branch or branches ;
3. *Motto:* "Nec deficit alter," or "Non deficit alter."

The last common ancestor of these four branches was the Rev. John Gregorie of Drumoak (No. VII., *ante*, p. 12), who died in 1650. It may, therefore, be assumed that in his time, if not earlier, armorial bearings with these characteristics were used by the family. A search among the Public Records of Scotland might result in the discovery of some deed bearing a seal which would confirm this conjecture.

The reasons for the adoption of the crest and motto must remain, at present, a mystery, but their connection is made sufficiently clear by the lines prefixed to this Chapter, to which they undoubtedly refer. The tree was the stem from which grew the golden branch—ever renewed—the passport to Hades, used by Æneas.† It must, therefore, have been a person of scholarly education who first suggested the adoption of the crest and motto,‡ and their date must accordingly be placed not earlier than the settlement of James Gregorie (No. VI.) in Aberdeen in the latter half of the sixteenth century. If a conjecture may be hazarded, it seems a plausible suggestion that the prominent position of this James Gregorie amongst his fellow citizens would have led him to assume armorial bearings for use in the civic pageants

---

* The substantial agreement of this seal with the devices adopted in three acknowledged branches of the family seems to put the identity of the James Gregorie, in whose name the letter so sealed was written, with the above-mentioned Professor James Gregorie beyond doubt. One or two expressions used in the letter tend to confirm this view.

† Cf. *Dante Purgatorio*, Canto I. *ad fin.*
  "O maraviglia ! chè qual egli scelse
  L'umile pianta, cotal si rinacque
  Subitamente là, ond' ei la svelse."

‡ It is clear that, strictly, the motto should commence with "Non" rather than "Nec."

of the day, while, not being connected with the Court, he may
have considered it superfluous to obtain the formal sanction of
the Lyon King-of-Arms. It must be that while the arms were
founded upon the devices of our Highland forefathers or connections,
the crest and motto had some special significance. Some circumstance, or some hope, is probably represented by the tree with its
constantly renewed golden branch. If the tree adopted was a
fallen fir it may have indicated the state of fortunes of the Clan
Gregor. But, whatever may have been its original meaning, the
device is one of good omen; and, while the shield reminds its
wearers of a long history in the past, the motto encourages them
with hopes of a golden future.

NEC DEFICIT ALTER."

ADDENDA ET CORRIGENDA.

Page 2. line 9 from bottom, *add* note, "The American Branch (chapter V.) seem, at all events, for many years, to have used the 'y' termination."

,, 5. line 6 from bottom, *add* note, "For an account of this incident see below, p. 87."

,, 6. line 7 from top, *dele* "and."

,, ,, line 21 ,, *add* note, "see page 17."

,, 14. line 18 ,, for "£3,600" *read* "£3,800."

,, 16. line 21 ,, for "£333 6s. 8d." *read* "£3,333 6s. 8d."

,, 20. note, for "p. 44" *read* "p. 47."

,, 27. line 6 from bottom, for "contribution" *read* "contributions."

,, 30. line 5 from top, for "1661" *read* "1659."

,, ,, line 17 ,, for "twenty-two" *read* "twenty-four."

,, 55. The statement in the third paragraph is erroneous. The life of Rev. Robert Hall was written by Olinthus Gregory (1774-1841), a person in no way connected with the family now in question, and was published in 1833.

,, 63. line 3 from top, for "to" *read* "in."

www.ingramcontent.com/pod-product-compliance
Lightning Source LLC
Chambersburg PA
CBHW030436190426
43202CB00036B/1540